Collins
easy learning
Italian

in a click

Clelia Boscolo

HarperCollins Publishers
77-85 Fulham Palace Road
London W6 8JB
Great Britain

www.collinslanguage.com

First edition 2010

Reprint 10 9 8 7 6 5 4 3 2 1

© HarperCollins Publishers 2010

ISBN 978-0-00-733741-5

Collins® is a registered trademark of
HarperCollins Publishers Limited

A catalogue record for this book is available
from the British Library

Typeset by Q2AMedia

Audio material recorded and produced by
Networks SRL, Milan

Printed and Bound in China by Leo Paper
Products Ltd.

Editorial Director: Eva Martinez

Series Editor: Rob Scriven

Contents

Introduction

Welcome to *Collins Easy Learning Italian in a Click*. This is a new course which aims to give you all the skills you'll need to start understanding and using Italian quickly, easily and effectively in real situations.

This course is aimed at adult learners with no previous experience of Italian. We've thought about which situations would be most useful to you during a visit to Italy, and have created a course that embraces all the main scenarios a traveller would be likely to encounter, such as public transport, checking into a hotel, shopping, eating out, visiting a museum and going to a football match. There's a section on keeping in touch using your computer or phone, and also a unit devoted to finding your way around and asking for help if anything goes wrong.

Our approach is not to bombard you with too much grammar, but rather to let you listen to authentic dialogues set in useful situations, giving you the nuts and bolts of what's being said, then guiding you through carefully gauged practice exercises to increase your confidence.

The tools you need to succeed

The course has been designed to provide you with three essential tools in order to make your language learning experience a success. In your pack you'll find an activation code for the **online course**, this handy **book**, and an **audio CD**. You can use a combination of these whenever and wherever you are, making the course work for you.

The online course

www.collinslanguage.com/click provides you with a 12-unit online interactive language experience. Listen to a dialogue (and follow the words on-screen if you like) then study the new words and phrases before tackling some fun interactive games and exercises. You'll then also have the chance to perfect your pronunciation by recording your own voice (microphone not provided).

Your progress will be saved automatically as you advance through the course in order that every time you log in you can see how well you've done in each of the exercises and how much of the course you've completed so far. But don't worry – if at any point you want to improve on your original scores, there's always the opportunity to go back and have another go.

To access the online course simply go to www.collinslanguage.com/click and enter your personal activation code which you will find inside the front cover of this book.

The book

There will be times when it's not practical for you to be at a computer. There will also be times when you simply don't want to stare at the screen. For these times, this pocket-sized book contains the whole course for you in a handy portable format, so you can continue learning without the need for a computer. All of the content you need to learn Italian is right here in this book. Study the language and complete the exercises just as you would online.

When you want to check your answers, go to **www.collinslanguage.com/click** to download the answer key.

The audio CD

Use the audio CD to hear native Italian speakers engaging in dialogues set in real life situations and use it alongside the book in order to improve your listening comprehension skills. The audio CD can be downloaded to your mp3 player so that you can keep on learning even when you're on the move.

See the website at **www.collinslanguage.com/click** for the written transcript of all the spoken dialogues.

How it works

Italian in a Click is divided into 12 units with revision sections after Unit 6 and Unit 12. Each unit begins with a **Traveller's tip**, a short passage highlighting an area of Italian life and culture, offering you tips on what to expect when you visit the country.

Following a brief summary of the language structures you're about to study, we move straight on to the first dialogue, headed **Listen up**. Any tricky or useful vocabulary is then explained in the **Words and phrases** box (with accompanying audio online), then we go into a little more detail in **Unlocking the language**. Then it's over to you. **Your Turn** offers further practice of each structure and area of vocabulary encountered.

Halfway through each unit, you'll see that the cycle begins again with a fresh **Listen up**. This adds a different dimension to the material and scenario you've already looked at, and provides you with a new challenge in a slightly different situation.

Each unit ends with **Let's Recap**, in which you can check over the language you've used in the unit. The online version then gives you the chance to **record yourself** saying some of the most important vocabulary from the unit, to compare your pronunciation with that of a native speaker.

Collins Easy Learning Italian in a Click **aims to be fun, but at the same time to equip you with genuinely useful linguistic and cultural tools to make the most of your time in Italy. We hope you enjoy it! Good luck!**

Piacere!
Pleased to meet you

1

We'll look at greetings and how to introduce yourself and say where you're from. You'll also learn how to say where you're going on holiday, and for how long.

Traveller's tip

From the days of the Grand Tour, Italy has always been a popular destination for foreign visitors, and its popularity continues to this day.

Recently, even more people have started to travel to Italy, whether it be on a short city break, a whistle-stop tour of the major cities, or a fly-drive arrangement allowing them to spend a couple of weeks exploring the jewels of Pompeii and Sicily in the south, Venice and the dramatic Dolomites in the north, or Rome, Florence and the other ancient cities of Tuscany in the centre.

The rise of budget airlines, together with the drop in fares charged by long-distance operators, has made Italy much more accessible to the independent traveller. Internal flights, trains, car hire and accommodation can be booked online, and the increased availability of rural properties to rent by the day, week or month has opened up areas of the country previously little known to the overseas tourist. You can find more details about this type of trip by searching for **agriturismo** on the internet.

There are nearly 50,000 British citizens living in Italy, mainly in Tuscany but increasingly in other regions, too. Thousands of them have opted to buy an Italian property, either as a second home, to make the most of Italy's glorious weather, or to settle and enjoy its good food and relaxed lifestyle.

Whatever type of visit to Italy you're planning, you'll quickly discover the truth of the tourist-industry slogan **Italia: molto di più** – Italy: much more.

In this unit we'll be working with two useful structures, to allow us to introduce ourselves and to say where we're going.

Sono ...   I am ...
Vado a ...   I'm going to ...

Listen up 1

A British woman meets an Italian man just before they catch a flight to Bologna. You can follow the conversation below as you listen to it. Then on the next few pages you'll find a series of explanations and exercises linked to what you hear.

Michele	Salve.
Lyn	Buongiorno.
Michele	Va a Bologna?
Lyn	Sì, vado a Bologna.
Michele	Ah, anch'io. Mi chiamo Michele.
Lyn	Piacere. Io sono Lyn.
Michele	È inglese?
Lyn	No, sono scozzese. Sono di Glasgow.
Michele	Ah, Lei è di Glasgow.
Lyn	Lei è di Bologna?
Michele	No, sono di Padova, però lavoro a Bologna. È studentessa?
Lyn	Sì, sono studentessa di italiano e francese.
Michele	Va a Bologna per studiare l'italiano?
Lyn	Sì, ad un corso estivo.
Michele	Ottimo. Be', io vado al bar.
Lyn	D'accordo. Arrivederci.
Michele	Arrivederci.

Greetings and other useful words

salve, buongiorno	hello, good morning. You will also hear **ciao,** which can mean both 'hi' and 'bye'.
piacere	pleased to meet you
però	but. **Ma** can also be used.
ad un corso *m* estivo	on a summer course
ottimo	excellent/very good
anch'io	so am I/me too
be' ...	well ...
d'accordo	OK
arrivederci	goodbye, see you lateV

Verbs

(Lei) va a ...?	Are you going to ...?
Vado a ...	I'm going to ...
Mi chiamo ...	My name is ...
Sono (di) ...	I am (from) ...
(Lei) è ...?	Are you ...?
lavoro	I work
studiare	to study

Some nationalities

inglese	English
scozzese	Scottish
italiano/italiana	Italian *m/f*
francese	French

A few jobs/occupations

insegnante	teacher
artista	artist
studente/studentessa	student *m/f*

🔒 Unlocking the language 1

In this section we explain some of the words and expressions introduced in the dialogue

l'italiano/il bar

'the Italian language/the bar'. To say 'the' in Italian, we use the word **il** for a noun that is masculine, and **la** for one that is feminine. If a word begins with a vowel (a, e, i, o and u), we use **l'**. All nouns in Italian are considered either masculine or feminine. You will also see **lo** being used before certain masculine words – those beginning with the following letters: **z**, **gn**, **pn**, **ps**, **x**, and **s + another consonant**.

Sono scozzese/di Padova/studente/ studentessa

'I'm Scottish/from Padua/a student.' **Sono** ('I am') and **è** ('you are') are both parts of the verb **essere** ('to be'). **È** can also mean 'it is' (**è interessante**). The three parts don't look very alike because **essere** is an irregular verb. We'll see more on this later.

You can also see that 'I'm a student' is just **sono studente/studentessa**. You don't say 'a' before a job or occupation in Italian.

(Lei) è inglese/di Bologna/studente/ studentessa?

'Are you English/from Bologna/a student *m/f*?' **Lei** means 'you' but, as you will have noticed in the dialogue, it can often be omitted because the verb (in this case, **è**) makes it clear who is being referred to.

inglese *m/f* italiano *m*/italiana *f*

Notice that nationalities are spelt with a small letter, and that their endings may vary depending on whether the person is male or female.

Va a Bologna? Vado a Bologna

'Are you going to Bologna?' 'I'm going to Bologna.' **Vado** ('I'm going') and **va** ('you're going') are both parts of the verb **andare** ('to go'). Like **essere**, **andare** is an irregular verb.

✈ Your turn 1

Listen again to Listen Up 1. Are the following statements true or false? 🔵 1

1. They are travelling to Bari. ....

2. Lyn is English. ....

3. Michele works in Bologna. ....

Check your understanding. Can you answer these questions?

1. What does Lyn study? ....
2. Where is Michele going at the end of the conversation? ....

Find expressions in the dialogue to convey the following:

1. Good morning. ....
2. Pleased to meet you. ....
3. Me too. ....
4. Are you going to Bologna? ....
5. Yes, I'm going to Bologna. ....
6. Are you a student? ....
7. Yes, I'm a student of Italian and French. ....
8. See you later. ....

Pronunciation Tips

Italian pronunciation is generally straightforward, with each letter pronounced logically. Where there are difficulties, we'll give you guidance in the Pronunciation Tip section in each unit.

Mi chiamo Michele
In Italian **chi** and **che** are pronounced *kee* and *keh*.

Bologna *bo-lo-nya*
The Italian **gn** is pronounced *ny* – rather like the 'ni' in the English 'onion'. We'll do some more practice of this sound later.

Ask someone: ⊙ 2

1. Are you French?
2. Are you English?

Say the following in Italian: ⊙ 2

1. I am Italian.
2. I am from Bologna.
3. I am a student.

Listen to track 3 and then answer these questions: 3

1. What is the man's name? ....
2. Where is he from? ....
3. What is Anna's nationality? ....
4. What is her job? ....

....

Match the Italian expressions on the left with their meanings on the right:

1. Sono australiano/australiana.	Are you Irish?
2. Lavoro in un ufficio.	It's very interesting.
3. Vado al bar.	I'm a student *m/f* of Italian.
4. Sono studente/studentessa di italiano.	I'm Australian. *m/f*
5. È irlandese?	I'm going to the bar.
6. È molto interessante.	I work in an office.

 ## Listen up 2

Listen to Alberto and Beatrice talking about themselves, their work and their studies. 4

Alberto Buona sera. Sono Alberto. Sono italiano, di Salerno, però vivo e lavoro a Bologna. Sono insegnante di matematica. Sono anche studente di fotografia. Adesso vado a lezione di fotografia. Poi vado al ristorante con i miei compagni di classe.

Beatrice Salve, sono Beatrice. Sono italiana, di Firenze, però vivo a Roma. Non lavoro. Sono studentessa di storia. Adesso vado a lezione. Poi vado al bar con il mio ragazzo.

Words and phrases 2

buona sera	good afternoon/evening
vivo	I live
a	in (I live in Rome), to (I'm going to class)
insegnante di matematica	maths teacher
fotografia *f*	photography
lezione *f*	lesson
adesso	now
poi	later on/then
non lavoro	I don't work
storia *f*	history
ragazzo/ragazza	boyfriend/girlfriend
con i miei compagni di classe	with my classmates

Unlocking the language 2

vivo e lavoro   'I live and (I) work'. All verbs saying what I do ('I study', 'I travel', etc.) end in **–o** in Italian, even irregular verbs like **sono** and **vado**.

un bar/   Notice that the word for 'a' can be **un** or **una**. This
una lezione   depends on whether the noun it goes with is masculine (**un bar**) or feminine (**una lezione**). **Una** is shortened to **un'** before a vowel (**un'australiana**). You will also see **uno** before certain masculine words.

Un/una can also mean 'one' – see 'Numbers' on page 14.

Your turn 2

Say the following in Italian: ⊙ 5

1. Hello. . . . .
2. I am English. . . . .
3. I live in Bologna. . . . .
4. I am a student. (*Try both male and female*.) . . . .

Numbers

Learning the numbers allows you to do all sorts of things like understand prices, tell the time and even ask someone what bus to catch. Here are the numbers 1 to 12. We'll learn some more later on.

1	uno (*when it stands alone*)	**6**	sei
	un bar (*working with a masculine noun*)	**7**	sette
	una lezione (*working with a feminine noun*)	**8**	otto
2	due	**9**	nove
3	tre	**10**	dieci
4	quattro	**11**	undici
5	cinque	**12**	dodici

⚲ Your turn 3

Rewrite the following to create Italian numbers:

1. TTOO

....

2. DINUCI

....

3. EDU

....

4. NOU

....

5. ROTTQAU

....

6. ICIDE

....

7. NICUQE

....

8. IDODCI

....

9. ERT

....

10. EIS

....

11. NU

....

12. VONE

....

13. AUN

....

14. TTESE

....

· ·

Listen to track 6. In which order are the numbers 1-12 pronounced? ⊙ 6
Mark the order against the list of Italian numbers below:

uno ....

due ....

tre ....

quattro ....

cinque ....

sei ....

sette ....

otto ....

nove ....1.......

dieci ....

undici ....

dodici ....

There are two mistakes in the following text. Can you spot them?

Buongiorno. Sono Maria. Sono italiano. Vivo a Milano però sono Roma. Sono economista.

....

Below is the transcript from Listen Up 2 (track 4) but lots of words have been missed out. Using the vocabulary that you have learned so far, fill in the gaps to check you've understood Alberto and Beatrice's descriptions:

1. Buona sera. .... Alberto. Sono .... di Salerno, però

    vivo e lavoro a .... Sono insegnante di matematica. Sono anche

    .... di fotografia. Adesso .... a lezione di fotografia.

    Poi .... al ristorante con i miei compagni di ....

2. .... sono Beatrice. Sono .... di Firenze, però vivo a

    .... Non lavoro. .... studentessa di storia. Adesso

    .... a lezione. Poi .... al bar con il mio ragazzo.

🔄 Let's recap

Here's an opportunity for you to revise the language you've learned in this unit. Supply the correct option in each case:

1. Lei .... italiana?

    a. sono   **b.** va   **c.** è

2. No, non .... italiana.

    a. va   **b.** sono   **c.** vado

3. Lei .... a Bologna?

    a. vado   **b.** è   **c.** va

4. Sì, ... a Bologna.

    a. è   **b.** vado   **c.** sono

....

Write the numbers 1–12 in Italian. We've started you off:

1. uno
2. due
3. ....
4. ....
5. ....
6. ....
7. ....
8. ....
9. ....
10. ....
11. ....
12. ....

Dov'è ...?
Where is ...?

2

You'll learn how to find your way around using public transport, and to locate places you need to find. We'll also study how to say at what time things happen.

Traveller's tip

Public transport in Italy is efficient and excellent value for money. Local bus services – and, in some of the larger cities, tram and **la metro(politana)** (underground train) networks – have benefited from huge investment and visitors are often surprised at how cheap transport is when compared to their home countries.

One of the main advantages of the bus system in Italian cities is that there is generally one (very reasonable) fixed fare, however many stops you wish to travel. A single ticket will usually allow you to combine travel on several means of transport to reach your destination. Further savings can be made by buying a multi-journey ticket – **un abbonamento** – giving you, say, ten journeys for the price of eight.

Travelling between cities by train is a delight in modern, clean, comfortable trains which are also remarkably affordable. The national rail network, **FS**, has a number of inter-city jewels in its crown, notably the high-speed **AV** (**Alta Velocità**), the **Eurostar** and the **Eurostar City**, linking all the major cities.

Alitalia offers affordable services between all the major cities, with very frequent services between Rome and Milan in particular.

In all major cities and in most tourist localities you will find an **Ufficio Turistico** or an **Ente di promozione Turistica**, where friendly, knowledgeable and, by and large, English-speaking staff will be able to supply all kinds of information on public transport, accommodation, places to visit, and more. In many cases they will also be able to make bookings and sell you tickets.

In the last unit we met the verb for 'to be' – **essere** – which we used to say things about ourselves. Now we're going to use the same verb to say where things are located. We'll also learn the language you need to say at what time a bus or train leaves and arrives.

A che ora ...?   At what time ...?
Dov'è ...?   Where is ...?

Listen up 1

Now let's imagine ourselves in a few situations you might find   ⊙ 7
yourself in when you visit Italy. We've arrived in Italy and are outside
the airport looking to continue our journey to our destination. First we
need to ask where the bus stop is:

You	Salve.
Passer-by	Buongiorno.
You	Dov'è la fermata dell'autobus?
Passer-by	È lì, a destra.
You	Ah, sì. Grazie.
Passer-by	Prego.

Now we're in the city centre looking for the underground station.   ⊙ 8
A passer-by is telling us that it's in the main street:

You	Per favore, dov'è la stazione della metropolitana?
Passer-by	È nella via principale.
You	Mille grazie.
Passer-by	Prego.

Now we need to buy a ticket – just a one-way ticket for the first   ⊙ 9
journey:

You	Un biglietto di sola andata, per favore.
Clerk	Due euro.
You	Grazie.

We're going on a day trip to the historic town of Ferrara, but this time we need a return ticket:

You	Un biglietto per Ferrara, andata e ritorno. Quant'è?
Clerk	Sono dodici euro, per favore.
You	Mille grazie.
Clerk	Prego, arrivederci.
You	Arrivederci.

Pronunciation Tip

Accents
You will have noticed the accent on the word **è** and also on the word **lì** ('there'). As a general rule you should pronounce any vowel with an accent on it more heavily than other vowels in the word e.g. **dov'è** ('where is') is pronounced *doh-VEH* whereas, without the accent, **dove** ('where') would be *DOH-veh*.

In the case of **è**, the stress is there to differentiate it from the very important word **e**, which means 'and'.

❝❞ Words and phrases 1

Dov'è ...? È ...	Where is ...? It's ...
fermata *f* dell'autobus *m*	bus stop
lì/qui	there/here
a destra	on the right
(mille) grazie	thank you (very much) (lit. a thousand thanks)
stazione *f* della metropolitana *f*	underground station
via *f* principale	main street
Prego.	You're welcome.
biglietto *m*	ticket
(di) sola andata	single
(di) andata e ritorno	return
per favore	please
Quant'è?	How much is (it)?

Unlocking the language 1

Dov'è la fermata?	'Where**'s** the bus stop?' **Dov'è** is a shortened form of **dove è**. **Quant'è?** is shortened in the same way (**Quanto è?**)
a destra	'on the right'. To say 'on the left', you use **a sinistra**. 'Straight on' is **sempre dritto**.
È un euro/Sono due euro.	'It's one euro/two euros.' Notice that for something costing two euros or more, the seller will say **sono** (literally 'they are', rather than 'it is').
	Notice also that Italians do not say **euros** but rather always use **euro**.

 ## Your turn 1

True or false? You can check your answers to all of the exercises online at www.collinslanguage.com/click.

1. The single ticket was 3 euros ....

2. The return to Ferrara was 12 euros ....

Essere ('to be')

You already know from Unit 1 that **essere** is used for many purposes:

Sono Michele **Sono studentessa**
È di Bologna   **È inglese**

Now, from the dialogues above, you can add where something is and prices to this list. Let's look at this important verb in more detail:

sono	I am
è	you are, he/she/it is
sono	they are

Which part of the verb you use depends on who or what it is you are talking about. Try to remember to think about this every time you form a sentence. Which form do you need?

Match the photos with the Italian word for each form of transport:

1. l'autobus ....
2. la metropolitana ....
3. il taxi ....
4. il treno ....

a.

b.

c.

d.

Find expressions in the dialogue to convey the following:

1. Where is the bus stop? ....
2. Where is the metro station? ....
3. How much is it? ....
4. It's ten euros. (*remember: they are*) ....

Make sure you can also say the following:

1. hello
2. please
3. thank you
4. thank you very much
5. you're welcome
6. goodbye

Pronunciation Tip

biglietto
The Italian **gli** is pronounced like the 'lli' in the English 'million'.

beel-yeht-toh

Ask for the following tickets in Italian:

1. To Bologna, return, please.
2. a single ticket

. . . .

Now try and remember how to ask these two questions: 12

1. Where is the bus stop? ....
2. How much is it? ....

. . . .

Listen to the dialogue on track 13 and answer these questions: 13

1. Where does the person want to go? ....
2. What sort of ticket does she ask for? ....
3. How much does it cost? ....

. . . .

Rearrange the word order in these expressions so that they make sense:

1. favore di sola andata per un biglietto ....
2. stazione è dov' la? ....
3. euro dieci sono ....
4. principale nella via è ....

Listen up 2

At the bus station. Listen to this conversation and see how much   14
you can understand. The passenger wants to get a bus to the capital:

Passenger	A che ora parte l'autobus?
Assistant	Parte alle quattro e mezza.
Passenger	E a che ora arriva a Roma?
Assistant	Arriva alle sei meno un quarto, circa.
Passenger	Mille grazie.

Making enquiries at the railway station. This customer wants to go to the university town of Padova:

Customer	Buona sera.
Clerk	Buona sera.
Customer	A che ora parte il treno per Padova?
Clerk	Parte alle dieci.
Customer	E a che ora arriva a Padova?
Clerk	Arriva a Padova alle undici e cinque.
Customer	Quant'è?
Clerk	Sono sei euro solo andata, e undici euro andata e ritorno.
Customer	Benissimo. Grazie.
Clerk	Prego.

📣 Words and phrases 2

treno *m*	train
A che ora parte?	(At) What time does it leave?
Parte ...	It leaves/departs ...
A che ora arriva?	(At) What time does it arrive?
Arriva ...	It arrives ...
per Padova	for Padova
solo andata	just one way (alternative to **di sola andata**)
circa	approximately

🔒 Unlocking the language 2

benissimo — 'great/very well'. If you want to say something is *very* good or *very* expensive or *very* bad, add -**issimo** to the end. 'Good' is **buono**, so 'very good' is **buonissimo**. 'tall' is **alto**, so 'very tall' is **altissimo**. Don't forget you need to match the ending to that of the word you are describing.

Talking about times

The basic question you will need in order to inquire as to when something happens is **A che ora?** It literally means 'at what hour?' Then you can add a verb:

A che ora arriva?   At what time does it arrive?
Arriva alle undici.   It arrives at eleven o'clock.

Notice that the verb is the same in the question and the answer. You will also have noticed that 'at' is **alle**. This is the case for all times except 1 o'clock:

all'una   at one o'clock
alle due   at two o'clock
alle tre   at three o'clock

Here's how to say some more complex times:

alle undici e cinque   at 11.05 (lit. at 11 and 5)
alle undici e dieci   at 11.10
alle undici e un quarto at 11.15 (lit. at 11 and a quarter)
alle undici e mezza   at 11.30 (lit. at 11 and half)
alle dodici meno un quarto at 11.45 (lit. at 12 less a quarter)
alle dodici meno dieci   at 11.50 (lit. at 12 less 10)
alle dodici meno cinque at 11.55

So **e** matches the 'past' half of the English clock, and **meno** equates to minutes 'to' the next hour.

✈ Your turn 3

Match up the clock faces with the times shown beneath:

1. le cinque e un quarto ....

2. le sette meno un quarto ....

3. le undici e dieci ....

4. le nove ....

a.

b.

c.

d.

Write the following in full in Italian:

1. at 4.10 ....
2. at 6.15 ....
3. at 9.30 ....
4. at 10.45 ....
5. at 12.55 (be careful!) ....

Can you say the following in Italian? ⊙ 16

1. The train leaves at three o'clock.   2. The bus arrives at ten o'clock.

Listen to the dialogue on track 17 and answer these three questions: ⊙ 17

1. Where is the passenger going? ....
2. What time does the train leave? ....
3. What time does it get to its destination? ....

Using the prompts in brackets, answer the following questions in Italian:

1. Dov'è la stazione della metropolitana? (main street) ....
2. Quant'è un biglietto di sola andata? (4 euros) ....
3. A che ora parte il treno? (9.15) ....
4. A che ora arriva l'autobus? (9.50) ....

⟳ Let's recap

Use one of the following words to fill each of the gaps below:

parte	l'	arriva	che	ora
quant'	quarto	biglietto	dov'è	

1. .... la fermata dell'autobus?
2. A .... ora .... il treno per Roma?
3. Parte alle due meno un ....
4. A che ora .... a Roma?
5. A che .... parte .... autobus?
6. .... è un .... di andata e ritorno?

Un piccolo aiuto
A little help

We'll put together an essential survival kit, to cover any situations in which you might run into problems, from simply not understanding to more complex situations involving injury, loss of possessions etc.

Traveller's tip

Among the problems expressed by students of Italian are the notions that Italians talk much more quickly than speakers of English, and that regional accents can be hard to follow. It's a fact that accents from the south of the country tend to be more difficult to understand, as various letters and word-endings seem to be missed off. The speed issue may or may not be true, but it's inevitable that there will be times when you don't catch what's been said to you, so we're going to focus on a few expressions to make it clear that you haven't understood, to ask for repetitions, and so on.

It's fair to say that Italy is generally a safe, friendly and easy-going place to spend time, but in any city or country there will always be the minority element looking to pick your pocket or trick you in some way. We'll show you what you need to say if you've lost your passport, money etc.

Equally, there's no legislating for when illness can strike, at home or abroad. In a small emergency, an Italian chemist's, **una farmacia**, can supply many more medicines without a doctor's prescription than a UK one, including most antibiotics. **Il farmacista**, the pharmacist, will be able to give you advice and sell you the necessary medication. Chemists display a green cross outside their premises and, when they are closed, have information about the location and the opening times of duty chemist's.

In case the worst should happen and you do fall ill, we'll equip you with the basic language necessary to explain what's happened so that you can get the correct treatment.

In this unit, as well as focusing on situation-specific language, we'll dip briefly into the past tense to say what has happened. This is a one-off – the rest of the course returns to primarily present-tense language.

Ho perso il passaporto.   I've lost my passport.
Mi hanno rubato la borsetta.   I've had my handbag stolen.

We'll also have a look at the verb **potere** ('to be able' or 'can') – to ask questions like 'can you help me?'

Mi può aiutare?   Can you help me?

Listen up 1

Listen to the series of short expressions on tracks 18 and 19 covering problems of understanding, and then giving you some phrases to use if you get lost. From now on you will not see the transcript here in the book but you can always go online to access all of the transcripts at www.collinslanguage.com/click.

⊙ 18–19

Words and phrases 1

Come?	Pardon? (*not having heard*)
Può ripetere, per favore?	Can you repeat that, please?
più lentamente	more slowly
Non capisco.	I don't understand.
Non parlo italiano.	I don't speak Italian.
Parla inglese?	Do you speak English?
Sono straniero/a.	I'm a foreigner. *m/f*
Non sono di qui.	I'm not from here.
Me lo scrive, per favore?	Can you write it down for me, please?

scusi/mi scusi	sorry (excuse me) – **mi scusi** is a slightly more formal way of excusing yourself
Mi può aiutare?	Can you help me?
Aiuto!	Help!
Mi sono perso/a.	I'm lost. *m/f*
Dov'è la piazza principale?	Where's the main square?
Dov'è l'Hotel Centrale?	Where's the Hotel Centrale?
Dov'è il bagno?	Where's the toilet?
Per andare alla stazione ferroviaria?	Which way is it to the railway station?
Mi fa vedere sulla cartina dove sono?	Can you show me on the map where I am?

 ## Unlocking the language 1

capisco –
non capisco;
parlo – non parlo;
sono di qui –
non sono di qui

'I understand – I don't understand'; 'I speak – I don't speak'; 'I'm from here – I'm not from here'. In order to make any verb negative, you just put **non** before it.

Mi può aiutare?
Può ripetere?

Può ('you can' or 'can you?') is part of the verb **potere** ('to be able') and is very useful for asking if someone can do something. For the verb that comes after it, such as 'help' or 'repeat', just use the infinitive – the basic form you find in the dictionary – you don't need to do anything to it.

scusi

As well as the general **scusi**, or **mi scusi**, there are various ways of saying sorry that can be used both for attracting attention and for apologising:

Senti (informal) or **senta** (polite) can be used to attract attention.

Mi dispiace is used purely for apologising.

Sono straniero/a.
Mi sono perso/a.

In Unit 1 we saw that certain nationalities could end with either an **a** or an **o** (**italiano/a**) depending on whether the person being referred to is female or male. Here are two more examples of this. If you are female, use **straniera** and **persa**. If you are male, use **straniero** and **perso**.

Spend a few minutes listening again to Listen up 1, then see if you can remember expressions to convey the following. You can check your answers online at www.collinslanguage.com/click.

1. I don't understand. ....
2. Can you repeat that, please? ....
3. more slowly ....
4. I'm not from here. ....
5. Will you write it down for me, please? ....
6. Can you help me? ....

The Italian alphabet

◉ 20

There are only 21 letters in the Italian alphabet.

a	(ah)	**h**	(ak-kah)	**q**	(koo)	
b	(bee)	**i**	(ee, *like the beginning of the English word 'even'*)	**r**	(erre, *a bit like the English 'air raid', but trilled*)	
c	(*like 'chi' in the English word 'chips'*)	**l**	(ell-eh)	**s**	(ess-eh)	
d	(dee)					
e	(eh)	**m**	(emm-eh)	**t**	(tee)	
		n	(enn-eh)	**u**	(oo, *as in the English word 'hoover'*)	
f	(effe *like the first 4 letters of the English word 'effect'*)	**o**	(oh)	**v**	(vee *or* voo)	
g	(jee)	**p**	(pee)	**z**	(tzeh-tah)	

Foreign letters

These letters are only used in Italian in a word that has been 'borrowed' from another language, such as the words 'jogging', 'weekend' and 'yoga'.

j	(ee loon-gah)	**x**	(iks)
k	(kap-pah)	**y**	(ee greh-kah *or* ipsilon)
w	(voo dop-pyah)		

It would be useful to work out how to spell your name and where you live in Italian. Practise these out until you can do it without looking at the guide.

Pronunciation Tip

When writing in Italian, there's no difference between a statement and a question, except for the question mark:

Mi può aiutare. You can help me.

Mi può aiutare? Can you help me?

However, in the spoken form, the question will tend to raise its pitch at the end, just as it would in English. Try saying the expressions above a few times, first as a statement and then as a question.

 Your turn 2

How would you say the following in Italian? ⊙ 2 1

1. I'm lost (*spoken by a man*)
2. I'm lost (*spoken by a woman*)
3. I'm foreign (*spoken by a man*)
4. I'm foreign (*spoken by a woman*)

•••

Listen to the voices, and make sure you have understood the problems the people are describing: ⊙ 2 2

1. Where does the first person want to go? ....
2. Where is the second person from? ....

•••

Explaining your situation. Match the predicaments on the left with the English translations on the right:

1. Mi può aiutare?   Can you help me?
2. Vado a ...   I'm lost.
3. Non capisco.   I'm a foreigner.
4. Mi sono perso/a.   I'm going to ...
5. Sono straniero/a.   I don't understand.

Listen up 2

Al commissariato di polizia/At the police station. Listen to the dialogue between a tourist and a policeman. ⊙ 23

All'ospedale (Pronto Soccorso)/At the hospital (Accident and Emergency). Now listen to a tourist explaining his health condition at the A & E reception desk. ⊙ 24

If you want to see any of the dialogues written out, you can consult the CD transcript online at www.collinslanguage.com/click.

Words and phrases 2

Mi dica (pure).	What's the problem? (lit. 'Tell me.')
Mi hanno rubato la borsetta.	I've had my handbag stolen.
stamattina	this morning
Non ha visto nessuno?	You didn't see anyone?
Ho perso ...	I've lost ...
portafogli *m*	wallet
cellulare *m*	mobile phone
i soldi (m pl)	money
la chiave dell'albergo	hotel room key
Va bene.	Okay.
non si preoccupi	don't worry
chiamiamo	we'll call
consolato *m*	consulate
non c'è di che	not at all (an alternative to prego)
Compili questo modulo.	Fill out this form.
nome *m*	first name

cognome *m*	surname
indirizzo *m*	home address
cittadinanza *f*	nationality
Ho il braccio gonfio.	My arm is swollen. (lit. 'I have the arm swollen.')
Le fa male?/Mi fa male.	Does it hurt (you)?/It hurts (me).
medico *m/f*	doctor
Come si chiama? Mi chiamo …	What's your name? My name is …
essere in vacanza	to be on holiday
carta *f* per l'assistenza medica	health insurance card – if you are an EU citizen, get hold of a European Health Insurance Card before you travel to Italy.
ecco	here you are
si accomodi	sit down

🔒 Unlocking the language 2

Mi hanno rubato …	'I've had my … stolen.' Don't worry about the complicated structure: just learn **mi hanno rubato** (+ name of item) as a one-off.
Ho perso …	This is another past tense – again, just focus on the meaning rather than how it's formed. You can start your explanation with **ho perso** …, then list any items lost.
compili	'fill out'. **Compilare** is the verb 'to complete/fill out (a form)'. The speaker here is using a polite command form, as the two people do not know each other well.
Le fa male (il braccio)? Mi fa male (il braccio).	'Does it/your arm hurt? It/my arm hurts.' **Fa male** comes from **fare male** ('to hurt'). If it's needed, the suffering body part comes after the **fa male** in both question and statement.
Mi fa molto male	'It really hurts./It hurts very badly.' In Unit 2 you learned that **–issimo** can be added to the end of a word to mean 'very'. **Molto** is another way to say 'very'. e.g. **molto male** – 'very bad', **molto costoso** – 'very expensive'.

i soldi

'the money'. Money is plural in Italian, so rather than using **il**, you use **i**. If you wanted to say 'the squares' (**la piazza** is a feminine word) you would say **le** instead of **la**. Any **lo** or **l'** masculine words become **gli** when they are pluralised. You will notice as well that the word itself usually changes ending, often to match the **i**, **gli** or **le**: **la piazza** – **le piazze**, **il passaporto** – **i passaporti**. Italian words do not take an 's' in the plural the way English words do.

✈ Your turn 3

Match the following photos with the Italian words beneath:

1. la chiave . . . .
2. la borsetta . . . .
3. i soldi . . . .
4. la carta di credito . . . .
5. il cellulare . . . .
6. il portafogli . . . .

a. b. c.

d. e. f.

Listen again to the dialogues on Tracks 23 and 24 and find expressions to convey the following: ◉ 23 & 24

1. Can you help me, please?
2. I've had my handbag stolen.
3. I've lost my passport.
4. My arm is swollen.
5. It hurts.

Can you say the following in Italian? The language that you know from the dialogues has been rearranged slightly: ◉ 25

1. I've had my passport stolen.
2. I've lost my handbag.
3. This morning at ten o'clock.

Listen to these two people telling you what has happened to them and then answer the questions: ⊙ 26

1. What has been lost in the first instance? ....

2. What's the problem in the second situation? ....

○ Let's recap

In this unit we've set out a couple of usages of a past tense. There's no need to learn the tense yet, but the expressions themselves are handy to keep in mind. Here's a reminder:

Mi hanno rubato ...   I've had my ... stolen.

Ho perso ...   I've lost ...

We've also learned how to create negative sentences, how to use the plural, how to say 'very' and how to say that something hurts.

• •

The following sentences have their words in the wrong order. Can you rectify them?

1. favore aiutare può per mi? ....

2. dove fa vedere sulla sono cartina mi? ....

3. borsetta mi rubato la hanno ....

4. braccio mi molto il fa male ....

• •

Choose the correct option to complete each sentence:

1. Mi dà .... passaporto?

   a. di   **b.** la   **c.** il   **d.** una

2. Sono .... in vacanza.

   a. Roma   **b.** qui   **c.** lì   **d.** qua

3. Compili .... modulo.

   a. questa   **b.** questo   **c.** queste   **d.** questi

4. Le .... molto male?

   a. braccio   **b.** fa   **c.** c'è   **d.** problema

All'hotel
At the hotel

We'll cover the language you'll need to check into a hotel in Italy and discover what facilities it has to offer. We'll also be taking a look at some of the different types of places to stay in Italy.

Traveller's tip

Every year, thousands of us head to Italy seeking sunshine, good food and drink, culture and relaxation.

Most hotel and tourism staff speak some English. However, there's a real achievement in speaking some Italian on holiday, and Italians will be delighted you've made an effort to learn their language. Here are some of the key words in considering accommodation.

On a modest budget, **una pensione** or **un bed & breakfast** could be for you – small establishments, often family-run, sometimes with meals, usually with breakfast and private bathroom, but occasionally without. Facilities can be basic, and credit cards are sometimes not accepted.

Backpackers should look out for **un ostello (della gioventù)**, 'a (youth) hostel'. Expect a multicultural environment and a lively time for a very reasonable price.

Un albergo and **un hotel** are both words for 'hotel'. Expect a higher level of service (and price!), usually with en-suite facilities, air-conditioning etc. Credit cards are widely accepted, and most Italian hotels take bookings online.

For an atmospheric, historical setting, you could try one of the many monasteries, convents, castles, stately homes or former palaces which have been converted into hotels. For nature lovers, **un agriturismo** ('farm holiday') usually offers decent accommodation with excellent food. Many spa towns (**terme**) offer accommodation and spa treatments in **centri benessere** ('wellbeing centres'). Have a look at these websites for more information: www.primitaly.it/agriturismi/uk.htm and www.stabilimenti-termali.com (only in Italian).

In this unit, we'll mainly be revising two structures we met earlier. They're both very useful for finding your way around and planning your time.

Dove sono ...? Where are ...? (Notice that this time we're asking about plural things. See below for examples.)

A che ora è ...? At what time is ...?

 Listen up 1

A couple arrive at an Italian hotel and check in. Listen to the dialogue and see how much you can understand. Remember that you can read all of the CD transcripts online at www.collinslanguage.com/click.

⊙ 27

Words and phrases 1

prenotazione *f*		booking
altro		something else/anything else
camera *f*		bedroom
una camera	singola	a single room
	doppia	a double room
	matrimoniale	with a double bed
	a due letti	with two beds (i.e. a twin room)
	con bagno	with an en-suite bathroom
	con doccia	with a shower

carta *f* di credito	credit card
ascensore *m*	lift
ristorante *m*	restaurant
al primo/quarto piano	on the first/fourth floor
colazione *f*, far colazione	breakfast, to have breakfast
cena *f*, cenare	dinner, to have dinner
stasera	this evening
andiamo in pizzeria	we're going to a pizza parlour
Le occorre altro?	Was there anything else?

🔓 Unlocking the language 1

Mi dà ...?	'Will you give me ...?' / 'May I have ...?' This is a good example of an instance where Italian speakers are very direct; this is perfectly polite, unlike in English where this sort of directness can sometimes seem rude.
Ecco	'Here you are'. This is the response to **Mi dà ...? Ecco** is a very useful little word – it can also be used in the following context: **ecco il treno** – 'here's the train'. Look it up in a dictionary to find other uses.
per dieci notti	'for ten nights'. When you're booking something for a period of time, remember to use **per** (+ **due ore, sette notti, tre giorni** ('days'), etc.)
siamo abbiamo andiamo	'we are', 'we have' 'we go/are going'. All of these verbs end in **-iamo**. This is your clue to the fact that they are all 'we' verbs – they all convey things done by 'us'.

✈ Your turn 1

Listen again to the dialogue on track 27 and check your understanding by answering these questions. You can check your answers online at www.collinslanguage.com/click. ⊙ 27

1. How many nights will they be staying? ....

2. What is the room number? ....

3. What time is breakfast? ....

4. What time is dinner? ....

Find expressions in the dialogue to convey the following:

1. We have a room booked. ....
2. for ten nights ....
3. your passport and your credit card ....
4. on the first floor ....
5. Dinner is at seven o'clock in the evening. ....
6. Is there anything else you need? ....
7. see you later ....

Numbers

Earlier on, we looked at the numbers from 1 to 12. Here's the next batch, from 13–99. Notice that each of them is just a single word:

13	tredici	**15**	quindici
14	quattordici	**16**	sedici

Notice the structure of the next few: 18 is composed of 'ten and eight'.

17	diciassette	**19**	diciannove
18	diciotto	**20**	venti

From 21 to 99, you'll see a structure of 'twenty one', 'twenty two', and so on. When the word for the tens is followed by **uno** or **otto**, it loses the last letter.

21	ventuno	**28**	ventotto	**50**	cinquanta
22	ventidue	**29**	ventinove	**60**	sessanta
23	ventitré	**30**	trenta	**70**	settanta
24	ventiquattro	**31**	trentuno	**80**	ottanta
25	venticinque	**32**	trentadue	**90**	novanta
26	ventisei	**40**	quaranta	**99**	novantanove
27	ventisette	**46**	quarantasei		

Be careful with the similarity between 60 and 70.

Write out the following numbers in full:

1. 32 ....
2. 44 ....
3. 59 ....
4. 60 ....
5. 67 ....
6. 76 ....
7. 81 ....
8. 93 ....

Pronunciation Tip

una cena fra amici (a dinner with friends)

The combination **ce** is pronounced like the beginning of the English word 'cheque'. Similarly, **ci** comes out like the beginning of the English 'chips'. If **ci** is followed by 'o' or 'a', it sounds like the beginning of 'chop' or 'cha-cha-cha'.

Try some more:

camere sedici e diciotto con doccia rooms 16 and 18, with shower

Arrivederci See you later

Using the language you've learned in this unit, think about arriving at a hotel, but this time with slightly different requirements. How would you say the following? Listening to track 28 will help you with this activity: ⊙ 28

1. A single room with a shower. ....
2. A double room with an en-suite bathroom. ....
3. A twin room. ....
4. A room with a double bed. ....
5. A room for fourteen nights. ....

Listen to the guests on track 29 and see if you can understand their requirements: 29

1. What sort of room is mentioned in the first request? ....
2. How many nights will the second people be staying? ....
3. What bathroom facility is specified by the third speaker? ....

• •

Match the questions on the left with the answers on the right:

1. Mi dà il passaporto, per favore?   È alle otto.
2. Dov'è l'ascensore?   No, grazie.
3. A che ora è la colazione?   È qui a sinistra.
4. Le occorre altro?   Sì, ecco.

Listen up 2

Later the same day, Claire asks the earlier receptionist's male colleague to recommend a good pizzeria. Listen to their conversation.   30

Words and phrases 2

Come va?	How's it going?
domanda *f*	question
ceniamo	we have dinner
in via Nazionale	on Nazionale street
lontano	far
vicino	near/close by
a piedi	on foot

in fondo a	at the end of
chiude	it closes
tardi	late

Unlocking the language 2

Come va?	This is a handy little question, which can be used to enquire about someone's health, how things are going or how they are getting on with a specific task or activity: the English 'how's it going?' is possibly the broadest equivalent.
a venti metri/a dieci minuti	To say how far away something is (either in distance or in time), use the little word **a** – it equates to the notion of 'away' in English: **È a dieci chilometri/minuti**. 'It's ten kilometres/minutes (away).'
A che ora è la cena? È alle otto.	When you're asking at what time something happens, remember to begin the question with **a** ('at').
Mi dica.	Literally 'tell me' – this is used to invite someone to say what they are looking for or what they want. It's also the usual way to say 'can I help you?' in shops.
È lontano/vicino.	'It's far away/close by.'
Non si preoccupi.	'Don't worry.' This is quite a complex structure in Italian, but you can just learn it here as a set phrase.
una buona pizzeria Le pizze sono molto buone.	Did you notice the difference between the uses of the word 'good'? Adjectives (describing words) often change in Italian depending on *what* they are describing. **La pizzeria** is **buona** but **le pizze** ('the pizzas') are **buone**. For **il** words, use **buono**, and for **i** words, use **buoni**.

Can you say the following in Italian? Listen to track 31 to hear the correct answers. ⊙ 31

1. Is it far?

2. It's ten minutes away on foot.

3. The pizzas are very good.

• •

Listen to the short dialogues on track 32 and make sure you've understood what is being said. Listen out in particular for the following information: ⊙ 32

1. Where is the hotel, and how many minutes does it take to get there?..............

....

2. Is the lift on the left or the right, and how many metres away is it?................

....

• •

Looking at the map above, complete the directions:

- Per favore, dov'è la pizzeria?
- La pizzeria .... in .... a ....
  Nazionale, a ....

• •

The following dialogue has one mistake in each line. Use the language you've learned above and in previous units to work out what's wrong:

A: Buono sera. Dov'è la pizzeria?

B: Il pizzeria è in via Dante.

A: Mila grazie. È lontano?

B: No, è a fondo a via Dante, a sinistra.

A: Benissima. Buona sera.

B: A rivederci.

Study the following short dialogues based around what time events begin. They're just here for you to read, recognise and use for practice.

1. – A che ora **è** la cena?
   – **È** alle nove.

2. – A che ora **ceniamo?**
   – **Ceniamo** alle otto

3. – A che ora **chiude** la pizzeria?
   – **Chiude** alle due di notte.

Useful Tips

- Notice that the verb in the question is re-used in the answer! So even if you don't know exactly what form has been used, you can copy what you heard.

- Remember to use **a** at the beginning of a question involving time, and **alle** (or **all'**) when you answer.

- -

Finally, choose the correct option to complete each sentence:

1. Buongiorno. Abbiamo una ....
   a. cena   **b.** hotel   **c.** prenotazione   **d.** colazione

2. Il ristorante è .... destra.
   a. il   **b.** la   **c.** in   **d.** a

3. A che ora è la cena? È alle ....
   a. otto   **b.** una   **c.** mezzogiorno   **d.** sera

4. Com'è la pizza? È ....
   a. buona   **b.** buono   **c.** buoni   **d.** buone

Prendiamo un aperitivo
Out for an aperitif

5

We'll be looking at the popular Italian tradition of having a pre-dinner drink and a snack, **un aperitivo**, as well as learning how to order drinks in a bar.

Traveller's tip

One of the greatest pleasures during your time in Italy will be relaxing over a leisurely **aperitivo** and a few **stuzzichini** (appetizers) in a bar, taking your time to sample as wide a range as possible.

Traditionally, the evening meal was preceded by an aromatic drink, – which could be anywhere from non-alcoholic to refreshingly potent - whose purpose was to whet the appetite: **aperitivo** comes from the Latin *aperire*, to open, to begin the meal. More importantly, though, the **aperitivo** was a social occasion, an opportunity to meet and chat after the working day, sipping a glass of **vermouth** in one of Turin's stylish Baroque cafés, some chilled sparkling white wine (**un bianchino**) in Milan, or a **spritz** (prosecco, sparkling or soda water and Aperol or another liqueur) in Venice, Padua and the other cities of the North – east. Each would be accompanied by small dishes of crisps, olives, peanuts, pickled vegetables, **salatini** (salty biscuits), snack-sized pizzas,

pieces of **focaccia** and various **tartine** (canapés).

Nowadays it is not uncommon to find cocktails accompanied by much larger portions of cold and hot food served from a buffet, and for the **aperitivo** to last much longer and to practically replace the evening meal, particularly in Milan and other cities of the North. It is also quite usual for bars to pride themselves on their own exclusive (and secret) concoction, so it's worth asking for **un aperitivo della casa** if you fancy something totally different and new. Just make sure you specify whether you want it alcoholic, **alcolico**, or alcohol-free, **analcolico**.

We'll be using several useful new verbs in this unit. These are vital for ordering drinks and snacks.

C'è/Ci sono ...?   Is there/Are there ...?
Vorrei ...   I would like ...
Per me ...   For me ...

Listen up 1

A couple are in a bar and wondering what snacks to have with their aperitifs. Listen to their conversation with the waiter.

⊙ 33

Remember that you can go online to www.collinslanguage.com/click to access the written version of the dialogue.

Words and phrases 1

cameriere *m*/cameriera *f*	bartender *or* waiter/waitress
lista degli stuzzichini	appetizers menu
vediamo ...	let's see ...
Che cosa è questo?	What's this?
focaccia *f* farcita	small savoury-filled focaccia
prosciutto *m*	ham
tonno *m*	tuna
pomodoro *m*	tomato
Il fatto è che ...	The thing is that ...
vegetariano/a	vegetarian *m/f*
mangiare	to eat
tartina *f*	canapé
senza	without
carne *f*	meat
questo *m*/questa *f*	this (one)
questi *m*/queste *f*	these (ones)

formaggio *m*, al formaggio	cheese, with cheese
verdure (*f pl*), alle verdure	vegetables, with vegetables
pizzetta *f*	snack-sized pizza
Altro?	Anything else?
olive ascolane	large green olives stuffed with a meat-based filling, covered in egg and breadcrumbs and fried.
subito	right now (straight away)
bruschette *f pl* al tonno *m*	slices of crusty bread, toasted and flavoured with olive oil, garlic and a variety of toppings, like tuna, ham (**al prosciutto**), salami (**al salame**), mozzarella (**alla mozzarella**), etc.
un po' di	a bit of, a few
Da bere?	(What can I get you) to drink?
bicchiere *m* di vino *m* bianco frizzante	glass of white wine. **Bicchiere** is used for all drinks. **Bianco** is the word for 'white' (think of the English 'blank'). You can also order **vino rosso** (red) or **rosé** (rosé), and you can choose between **fermo** (not sparkling) or **frizzante** (sparkling).
analcolico/a	non-alcoholic. 'Alcoholic' is **alcolico/a**
della casa	house (wine, etc.)
Si accomodino, arrivo subito.	Sit down. I'll be right back.

🔓 Unlocking the language 1

C'è .../Ci sono ...(?)	'There is .../There are .../Is there ...?/Are there ...?' **C'è** is a combination of **ci** ('there') and **è** ('is'). It is used in a variety of contexts - in this case it is used to ask whether something is available (**C'è una lista?** 'Is there a menu?') and also to refer to the content of a snack (**C'è il prosciutto?** 'Does it contain ham?'). **Ci sono** is the plural ('they contain/there are/are there ...(?)')
Vorrei ...	This is part of the verb **volere** ('to want'), and is used here to order something to eat or drink. It is equivalent to 'I would like ...'
Per me ...	Another very straightforward way to order things: 'For me ...'

Match the photos with the names of stuzzichini. You can check your answers online at www.collinslanguage.com/click.

1. olive ascolane ....
2. pizzetta ....
3. tartine ....

a.   b.   c.

Find expressions in the dialogue in track 33 to convey the following: ⊙ 33

1. Is there an appetizers menu? ....

2. What is this? ....

3. I'm vegetarian. (*female*) ....

4. This one contains tuna and tomato. ....

5. I would like two cheese canapés. ....

6. Something to drink? ....

7. For me, a glass of white wine. ....

Pronunciation Tip

focaccia

As we saw earlier, **ci** and **ce** are pronounced like the 'chi' and 'che' in the English 'chips' and 'cheque'. If **ci** is followed by **o** or **a**, it sounds like the beginning of 'chop' or 'cha-cha-cha'. A double **c** means a longer 'ch' sound.

ecco, bruschetta, bicchiere

ca, co, cu, chi and **che** are pronounced *kah, koh, koo, kee* and *keh* respectively. A double **c** means a longer 'k' sound.

Now, using the language you've learned above, think about ordering some different appetizers and drinks. How would you say ...the following? Begin each order with vorrei ... ⊙ 34

1. three vegetable canapés ....

2. two tuna and tomato bruschettas ....

3. a bit of ham focaccia ....

4. two non-alcoholic aperitifs ....

5. a glass of red wine ....

Listen to these three food and drink orders, and answer the questions: ◉ 35

1. How many canapés of each type does the first speaker order? ....

....

2. What does the man order with the focaccia? ....

....

3. Is it two non-alcoholic aperitifs and a glass of white wine that the final

customer wants? ....

....

Listen again to track 33 and see if you can identify the following appetizers from their photos:

| 1. | 2. | 3. |

1. ....

2. ....

3. ....

Match the expressions on the left with their translations on the right:

1. In queste c'è la carne?   with a bit of focaccia

2. con un po' di focaccia   three aperitifs

3. Vorrei una bruschetta al formaggio. Have these got meat in them?

4. tre aperitivi   I would like a cheese bruschetta.

Listen up 2

In the next bar, it's time to order some drinks. Listen to the dialogue and see how much you can understand.

⊙ 36

Words and phrases 2

Prego ...	Can I help you? (An alternative to **mi dica** (**pure**).) You already know **prego** as 'you're welcome'.
birra *f* piccola	a small beer. The alternatives to **piccola** are **media** (medium) and **grande** (large).
caffé *m* decaffeinato	decaffeinated coffee
macchiato	with a dash of milk
Che stuzzichini ci sono?	What appetizers are there?
Ci sono ...	There are ...
patatine *f pl*	crisps
olive *f pl*	olives
noccioline *f pl*	peanuts
salatini *m pl*	small savoury biscuits
cipolline *f pl*	small pickled onions

una birra piccola

Did you notice that in Italian the adjective usually comes after the word that it is describing? 'A beer small', 'a room comfortable' and so on.

un caffé

The most popular coffee orders in Italy are **un caffé/un espresso** (which both mean 'an espresso'), **un caffé macchiato** (as above, but with a small amount of milk) and **un caffé corretto** (an espresso with a shot of grappa). If you want filter coffee, ask for **un caffé americano**. The nearest thing to white coffee is **un cappuccino**.

Sono allergico/a a ...

'I'm allergic to ...' This is a very useful thing to be able to say if you do have allergies. If you want to talk about someone else's allergy you would say **è allergico/a a ...**

✈ Your turn 2

Find the appetizers and drinks hidden in these anagrams:

1. lineocinoc ....
2. rabir ....
3. veilo ....
4. linepolci ....
5. novi ....
6. tinarat ....
7. forgiomag ....
8. affcé ....

Can you say the following in Italian?   37

1. What appetizers are there? ....
2. A few olives, please. ....

Listen to these two short dialogues and make sure you've understood what is being said. Focus on the following points:

1. What hot drinks are ordered in the first exchange? ....
    ....

2. In the second exchange, is the order for white wine and olives or red wine and peanuts? ....
    ....

. . . .

Fill in the gaps in this conversation between a barman and a customer. We've given you some first letters:

Cameriere	Mi d..........., signora.
Cliente	Un aperitivo e un po' di patatine, per favore.
Cameriere	A...........?
Cliente	Sì, anche due olive ascolane.
Cameriere	E d........... b..........., un aperitivo alcolico?
Cliente	Sì, un bicchiere di vino bianco.

 ## Let's recap

Remember that the main points in this unit were:

1. Asking if someone has something – **C'è una lista?**

2. Asking if an appetizer contains something – **C'è la carne?**

3. Ordering food and drinks – **Vorrei .../Per me un po' di ...**

. . . .

Now see how good your memory is. Can you give the Italian names for these appetizers?

1.

....

2.

....

3.

....

4.

....

5.

....

6.

....

Choose the correct option to complete each sentence:

1. Buona sera. Vorrei due .... al tonno.

   a. ristorante   **b.** tartine   **c.** pizzetta   **d.** focaccia

2. Nella focaccia non .... carne.

   a. è   **b.** sono   **c.** ci sono   **d.** c'è

3. .... vegetariano.

   a. Sono   **b.** C'è   **c.** Ci sono   **d.** Vorrei

4. Per me un .... macchiato, per favore.

   a. birra   **b.** vino   **c.** caffé   **d.** aperitivo

Al ristorante
In the restaurant

6

We'll be focusing on the restaurant experience in Italy, looking at the language you'll need to order what you want, as well as highlighting some of the regional delicacies you might fancy trying.

Sitting down to a meal in Italy – whether in a top-class restaurant or a humble set-menu trattoria – is not an experience to be rushed. Whilst relatively little importance is attached to breakfast, Italians have traditionally relished the long lunch or dinner as something to be enjoyed by the whole family.

Many visitors' first taste of Italian food in Italy could well be a **menù turistico**, a daily menu offering three multi-choice courses, including certain drinks, for around €10–12.

Higher up the market, famous Italian chefs and restaurants, both in Italy and in the UK have been making waves internationally for the excellence and originality of their cuisine.

If you're eating out, you will notice a range of techniques for diners to attract waiters' attention: raising arms, clicking fingers, even whistling! These are fascinating to observe, but you wouldn't necessarily want to copy them!

Each region of Italy is fiercely and justifiably proud of its local dishes. In the south, rich dishes favouring olive oil, garlic, fish and tomatoes are typical, while the north west specialises in **risotto** and other rice dishes. The northern region of Emilia Romagna is justly famous for its **prosciutto di Parma** and **parmigiano reggiano**, as well as for its **pasta** dishes, while in the centre of the country you can enjoy excellent meat dishes, ranging from the succulent **fiorentina** to the equally tantalising **abbacchio**.

With Italy's international reputation for wine production, you can be assured of a fine selection of robust reds, chilled whites, fruity rosés or sparkling **spumante**, all affordably priced, whichever area you're visiting. **Buon appetito!**

In this unit we'll be sitting down to a three-course lunch and using several useful new structures along the way. We'll learn more about the conventions of ordering food

(Che) cos'è ...?	What is ...?
Prendo ...	I'll have ...

Listen up 1

A couple go into a restaurant for a set-menu lunch. Listen to the dialogue and see how much you can understand.

⊙ 39

Remember you can read the transcript for all of the CD tracks online at www.collinslanguage.com/click.

Words and phrases 1

C'è un tavolo per due?	Is there a table for two?
tavolo *m*	table
da questa parte	this way
di primo	as a starter (lit. 'of the first (course)').
di secondo	for the main course (lit. 'of the second (course)')
stracciatella *f*	clear soup, made from meat stock, eggs and parmesan cheese
o	or
prosciutto *m*	ham, available as **crudo** (the generic name for Parma ham) or **cotto** ('cooked').
melone *m*	melon
minestra *f*	soup
uovo *m*/uova *f pl*	egg/eggs
Per Lei?	For you?

pollo *m* arrosto	roast chicken
patatine fritte *f pl*	fried potatoes, chips
fagiolini *m*	green beans
braciola *f* ai ferri	grilled chop
pesce *m*	fish
maiale *m*	pork, pig
frutti di mare *m*	seafood. **Risotto ai frutti di mare** is a common dish in Italy, but you will also find risotto cooked in a variety of other ways: **alla milanese** (with saffron, parmesan cheese and white wine); **ai funghi** (with mushrooms); agli asparagi (with asparagus)
Da bere?	What would you like to drink? (lit. to drink?)
acqua *f* minerale naturale	still mineral water. **Frizzante** is fizzy.

🔓 Unlocking the language 1

(Che) cos'è ...?   'What is ...?' We saw this first in Unit 5. You can use this useful expression with or without **che** (*ke*). In full it would be **(Che) cosa** (what) **è** (is)**?**

(Io) Prendo ...   'I'll have ...' **Prendo** literally means 'I'll take ...'. You can also use it to say 'I'll take the bus' – **Prendo l'autobus**. The **io** (meaning 'I') is not necessary but is there for emphasis – 'as for me, I'll have ...'

risotto ai frutti di mare   'seafood risotto'. **ai** is a combination of **a** ('of') and **i** (masculine plural 'the' to match 'the fruits of the sea'). It is shortened for ease of speech. Here is a list of how to form all of the possible combinations:

a + **il** = **al**   **a** + **i** = **ai**

a + **la** = **alla**   **a** + **le** = **alle**

a + **lo** = **allo**   **a** + **gli** = **agli**

a + **l'** = **all'**

Now that you know these, you will see them everywhere. Whenever you notice one in upcoming dialogues, think about how it is formed.

Listen again to track 39 and find expressions to convey the following. Afterwards, you can check your answers online at www.collinslanguage.com/click. 39

1. Is there a table for two? ....

2. As a starter ... .

3. For the main course ....

4. What is *stracciatella*? ....

5. I'll have the ham and melon. ....

6. Something to drink? ....

7. Two glasses of red wine ....

> ## Pronunciation Tip
> **secondo, minestra, stracciatella**
> **risotto**
>
> The Italian **s** has two sounds: at the beginning of words (**secondo**) and when followed by another consonant (**minestra**) it sounds like the 's' in 'start'. If it is between two vowels (**risotto**), it sounds like the 's' in 'rose' – more like an English 'z': *ree-zot-toh*

Now, using the language you've learned above, think about ordering a range of different starters, main courses and drinks. How would you say the following? Begin each order with prendo ... 40

| 1. | 2. | 3. | 4. | 5. |

1. the chicken with French fries ....

2. the grilled chop ....

3. the soup with eggs and cheese ....

4. the seafood risotto ....

5. a glass of white wine ....

In Unit 5 you also learned to use per me and vorrei to order food and drinks.
These could both be used in any of the phrases in the previous exercise.
Try saying aloud the orders, using either per me or vorrei instead.

··

Listen to these people ordering a meal, and write true or false   4 1
next to the three statements:

1. The man orders the ham and melon and the risotto ....

2. The woman orders the soup and the chicken ....

3. They would also like two beers and a bottle of wine ....

··

Match the expressions in the left-hand column with their 'continuations'
on the right:

1. Di primo c'è   acqua minerale naturale.

2. Da bere vorrei   per quattro?

3. Di secondo prendo   minestra o lasagne.

4. C'è un tavolo   pollo ai ferri.

Listen up 2

The couple have finished their main courses.
Their waiter asks them what they'd like next.   4 2
Listen and see how much you can understand.

Remember to access the transcript online if you
think it will help you.

Words and phrases 2

Va bene?	Here the meaning is 'How was the meal?' Generally it is used to mean 'Is it going well?', 'How are things?' and 'Okay?'
tutto	everything

dolce *m*	dessert
gelato *m*	ice cream
macedonia *f*	fruit salad. The word for fruit is **frutta** – you saw this word in the previous dialogue as **frutti di mare** – fruits of the sea.
torta *f*	cake
al cioccolato *m*	chocolate-flavoured
alla vaniglia *f*	vanilla-flavoured
alla fragola *f*	strawberry-flavoured
panna *f* cotta	cream pudding
senta	'excuse me' (lit. hear!) A polite way of attracting someone's attention.
conto *m*	the bill
Mi porta il conto?	Can I have the bill, please? (lit. Will you bring me the bill?)
Tenga il resto.	Keep the change.

Unlocking the language 2

C'è / Non c'è

Remember that the way of making a verb negative is simply to put **non** before it: **c'è** – 'there is'; **non c'è** – 'there isn't'.

torta al cioccolato
gelato alla vaniglia

We learned earlier in this unit that the word **a** is always combined with 'the'. This dialogue has lots more examples of this rule. Did you spot them?

Tenga il resto.

This is a command form, but has a polite tone to it. There's no obligation to leave a tip in Italian bars and restaurants (people often just leave a couple of coins) but there is no harm in leaving 5–10% if you've enjoyed your meal.

Mi porta il conto?

This is the standard way to ask if you can have the bill, but you can also say **il conto, per favore** – 'the bill/ check, please'.

Find the desserts and flavours hidden in these anagrams:

1. ategol ....
2. otart ....
3. apantancot ....
4. golaraf ....
5. avangili ....
6. madeincao ....

Can you say the following in Italian? 4 3

1. Nothing for me
2. I'll have an espresso
3. Can I have the bill, please?

Listen to these short dialogues, and identify which of the options are being asked for: 4 4

1. Does the customer ask for:
   a. a coffee and a vanilla ice cream
   b. a cream pudding and a strawberry ice cream
   c. a chocolate ice cream and some fruit?

2. Does the customer ask for:
   a. two black coffees
   b. one white coffee
   c. one espresso and a coffee with a dash of milk?

Look back at Unit 5 if you have forgotten the vocabulary for coffee.

Each of the statements below has its words in the wrong order. Use the language you've learned in this and previous units to sort them out:

1. favore conto porta il per mi? ....

2. conto il ecco ....

3. trenta sono signore euro ....

4. resto il tenga ....

Let's recap

The main points in this unit have been:

1. establishing what there is on a desserts menu – **C'è il gelato al cioccolato?**

2. stating preferences/orders – **Prendo il risotto/Prendo la torta/Per me un caffè**.

3. looking at restaurant conventions – **un tavolo per due; di primo/ secondo/dolce ...; mi porta il conto?**

• •

Now see how good your memory is. Can you give the Italian names for these dishes?

1. soup with eggs and parmesan ....

2. ham and melon ....

3. roast chicken with fries ....

4. grilled chop ....

5. cream pudding ....

6. chocolate cake ....

Choose the correct option to complete each sentence:

1. .... primo c'è stracciatella o prosciutto e melone.

   a. Per   **b.** Da   **c.** La   **d.** Di

2. .... dolce?

   a. Sono   **b.** Un   **c.** Ha   **d.** C'è

3. .... un espresso, per favore.

   a. Sono   **b.** Per me   **c.** Ho   **d.** Due

4. Tenga il ....

   a. tavolo   **b.** ristorante   **c.** conto   **d.** resto

Ripasso 1
Revision 1

About yourself

Can you remember how to build up the following information about yourself in Italian, using the verb essere?

- I am (name)

- I am (nationality) – remember to use the masculine or feminine ending of the nationality word as appropriate

- I am from (*town*)

- I am (*job/occupation*) – remember not to use an equivalent of 'a' before the job

- I am (*characteristics*) – look up some new adjectives to describe your appearance and personality. Remember to check if you need to change the ending of any descriptive words.

Spelling

Refer to the alphabet in Unit 3, and practise spelling out your name and address. It's a good idea to keep coming back to this, and to take as many opportunities as possible to spell words out.

Listen up

Listen to the voicemail left by the manager of an Italian property company for an English-speaking client, Mr Dobson. Then answer the questions below:

⊙ 45

1. What is the caller's full name? ....

2. Which company does he represent? ....

3. On what street is the house located, and at what number? ....

4. Who has the key – what is her full name? ....

5. At what street number, and on what side of the road, is the office located? ....

....

6. What is her nationality and what second language does she speak? ....

....

7. What are her working hours? ....

Speak up

You might like to think about where you are going on holiday. ⊙ 4 6
How would you say the following in Italian?

1. Are you going to Bologna?

2. Yes, I'm going to Bologna.

3. Are you going to Italy?

4. No, I'm not going to Italy.

Where is …?

Think about places and items in your life, and where they're located. Perhaps your local bar is at the end of the street on the left, or the railway station is 'near here'. Practise asking 'where is…?' and replying 'it's…' using **è.**

At what time?

Look again at the structures in Unit 2 for saying at what exact time things happen (trains departing, etc.) as well as the time of day. Now try and remember how you would say the following sentences in Italian:

1. At what time does the train for Rome arrive?

2. It arrives at three o'clock.

3. At what time does the bus to Venice leave?

4. It leaves at half past ten.

Numbers

Revise the numbers from 0 to 99 carefully. Try to spot and memorise the patterns in clusters (e.g. the teens, twenties).

Now try and say out loud the following Italian numbers: ⊙ 4 7

1. 16	**5.** 31	**9.** 80
2. 20	**6.** 56	**10.** 94
3. 27	**7.** 67	
4. 30	**8.** 78	

Parlando con la gente
Talking to people

7

We'll go deeper into some of the structures we've already covered, to allow you to engage more fully in conversations with people you meet. We'll also learn how to speak to people in a less formal way.

Traveller's tip

One of the trickiest barriers to overcome when you're learning Italian and using it to talk to people is the range of different ways of saying 'you'.

In standard modern English, there is just one form: whether you're talking to one person or ten, to a prime minister or a child, the word is simply 'you'.

In Italian it's different. So far in this course, we've used what is known as the formal or polite form, generally used when you don't know someone very well and you want to be respectful. This has been characterised by the word **Lei** (polite 'you') and a particular verb form to go with it.

In this unit we'll turn our attention to the informal, 'friendly' form, used with someone your age or younger, with whom you feel comfortable and whom you now feel you know a bit better. This is often known as the **tu** form (= informal 'you').

With practice you'll know instinctively which form to use. It's safer to start with the polite form so as not to risk offending anyone, but Italians will understand that you are not being intentionally rude if you use the wrong form. They will often put you at your ease by saying **dammi del tu** ('speak to me informally') or **possiamo darci del tu** ('we can treat each other as **tu'**).

In this unit we'll be comparing formal and informal ways of addressing people. We'll also be revising some earlier structures and adapting them.

Vai in centro?	Are you going to the centre?
Quanti anni hai?	How old are you?
Sei studente/inglese?	Are you a student/English?

 ## Listen up 1

Tom and Linda are on the bus when they bump into Matteo, a man they met the previous day. Listen to their conversation. Remember that you can view the transcript for all of the audio tracks at www.collinslanguage.com/click.

 48

Words and phrases 1

Possiamo darci del tu.	We can treat each other as **tu**.
certo	of course
devo	I have to/must
fare spese	to do some shopping
anch'io	me too
prendere qualcosa da bere	to have something to drink
buona idea	good idea
Cosa prendi?	What will you have?

Offro io.	It's my treat, I'm buying (lit. 'I offer')
Vuoi ...?	Do you want ...? (*informal 'you'*)
oggi	today
compleanno *m*	birthday
auguri	greetings, best wishes
se non sono indiscreto	if you don't mind my asking
anno	year
Quanti anni hai?	How old are you?
Ho ventitré anni.	I'm 23.
Sono il vecchio del gruppo.	I'm the old one in the group.
Non ti preoccupare.	Don't worry (we heard the formal **non si preoccupi** in previous units).
Cin cin!	Cheers! You will also hear **Salute**! (lit. 'health')

🔓 Unlocking the language 1

Vai in centro?
Prendi qualcosa da bere?

We're now starting to focus on the informal style of each verb. Generally, this is just the formal 'you' style we've learned (**prende**, **ha**, **va**) but ending with an **-i** (**prendi**, **hai**, **vai**). We'll do plenty more practice, so don't worry if it's a bit confusing at first.

il compleanno di Linda

There's no apostrophe in Italian to allow you to say something like 'Linda's birthday'. Instead, you have to say 'the birthday of Linda'.

Quanti anni hai?
Ho ventitré anni.

To ask and tell your age in Italian, you don't talk about being 23, but rather having 23 years. So you use the verb **avere** – 'How many years do you have? I have 23 years.'

Find expressions in the dialogue (track 48) to convey the following. You can check your answers by going online to www.collinslanguage.com/click. ⊙ 48

1. We can treat each other as **tu** ....

2. Are you going to the centre? ....

3. Do you want something to drink? ....

4. It's my treat. ....

5. Best wishes. ....

6. Don't worry. ....

> ## Pronunciation Tip
>
> **offro io, non ti preoccupare, oggi, compleanno**
>
> Try to stress every double consonant in Italian by making the sound a little bit longer. This is easier with shorter words, but at the end of a word like **compleanno**, it's easy to slip into a short English **n**. Try saying **oggi è il compleanno di Alessandro** (today is Alessandro's birthday), really stressing the double consonants. This is a simple point, but often overlooked.

Speaking informally and using prendere, how would you ask for the following? ⊙ 49

1. Will you have a beer?

2. Will you have a glass of wine?

3. Will you have an aperitif?

Listen to the voices on track 50, and focus on the following questions: ⊙ 50

1. How old is the first speaker? ....

2. The next speaker says 'you are 15' – is the address formal or informal? ....

3. How old is the third speaker? ....

Fill in the gaps below, supplying the formal equivalent of each verb. We've given you one to start off:

Informal	Formal
1. Quanti anni hai?	Quanti anni ha?
2. Mi dai una birra?	....
3. Mi puoi aiutare?	....
4. Vai in centro?	....
5. Sei italiano?	....

 ## Listen up 2

Danny chats to Sofia, an Italian girl, in the park. Listen to their conversation.

 51

 ## Words and phrases 2

scusa	excuse me – informal version of scusi. Don't get confused by this – usually –**i** would signify a **tu** (informal) conversation but this is a command so it's the opposite way around!
sei	you are (informal, from **essere**)
perso/a	lost *m/f*
va tutto bene	everything's fine
vero?	right? (lit. true?)
canadese *m/f*	Canadian
essere in vacanza	to be on holiday. To go on holiday is **andare in vacanza**
studio	I study (from **studiare**)
scuola *f* di lingue	language school
parli	you speak (informal, from **parlare**)

esercitarsi	to practise
allora	then
insegnante *m/f*	teacher
guida *m/f*	person working as a guide
lavoro *m*	job/work
lavorare	to work
poco tempo *m* libero	very little free time
preferisco	I prefer
ordinare	to order (drinks/food)
qualcosa	something
succo *m* d'arancia	orange juice (lit. 'juice of orange')
quanto Le devo?	How much do I owe you?

 ## Unlocking the language 2

Va tutto bene

This could be the answer to **Come va?** which we came across earlier. It literally means 'everything is going fine'.

sei

This is the informal 'you' form of **essere**. Let's summarise this verb:

sono – I am
sei – you are (informal)
è – you are (formal), he is, she is, it is
siamo – we are
sono – they are

Ti sei perso?
Sei in vacanza?
Sei studente.
Non sei di qui.
C'è il prosciutto?
Dov'è la stazione?
Sono dodici euro.
Siamo Graham e Linda.
Sono canadese.
Sono insegnante e guida turistica.

These are examples of the various uses of **essere** we have come across so far. Study them carefully and check that you can understand why each form of **essere** is used. Can you make up some examples of your own?

I like ...

In Italian, rather than saying 'I like ...', you say '... pleases me':

Mi piace ...

In *Listen Up 2* we saw the following example: **Mi piace lavorare** 'I like working/to work'.
Piacere can also work with things: **Mi piace il vino** 'I like wine'.

If you want to ask someone if they like something you can use the following structure:
Le piace il vino? (*formal*) or **Ti piace il vino?** (*informal*) 'Do you like wine?'
A likely response might be: **Sì, mi piace molto** 'Yes, I really like it'.

Your turn 2

Here are some anagrams of some informal (ending in -i) Italian verbs for you to unravel:

1. lirap ....

2. nerdip ....

3. ouvi ....

4. ahi ....

5. iav ....

6. ies ....

Can you say the following in Italian? We're using the informal form. 52

1. Are you on holiday?

2. I'm on holiday.

3. Everything's fine.

4. Don't worry.

Listen to descriptions a, b, c and d on Track 53 and write the correct letter under the corresponding picture below:  53

1.

....

2.

....

3.

....

4.

....

Below are some formal (polite) questions. Use the language you've learned in this unit to change each verb to the informal style:

1. Prende un caffè? ....

2. Ha molto tempo libero? ....

3. È in vacanza? ....

4. Va in centro? ....

In this unit we've looked at the difference between polite and informal ways of addressing people. We've also studied the way to ask and state how old someone is. Here are some model sentences to help you remember:

È canadese? (*polite*)
Sei canadese? (*informal*)

Mi può aiutare? (*polite*)
Mi puoi aiutare? (*informal*)

Quanti anni ha? (*polite*)
Quanti anni hai? (*informal*)

• •

Now see how good your memory is for numbers. Each of the numbers below is misspelt. Try and spot the error, then practise saying the corrected version

1. 33   trientatré
2. 44   cuarantaquattro
3. 55   quinquantacinque
4. 66   settantasei

• •

Choose the correct option to complete each sentence with an informal tu word:

1. . . . . nervoso oggi.
   a. Sei   **b.** È   **c.** Va   **d.** So

2. . . . . 23 anni.
   a. Sei   **b.** Hai   **c.** Ha   **d.** È

3. . . . . andare al bar.
   a. Ha   **b.** Hai   **c.** Vuole   **d.** Vuoi

4. . . . . andare in centro.
   a. Sono   **b.** Puoi   **c.** Può   **d.** Potere

Fare spese
Out shopping

8

We'll cover the language you'll need when you go out shopping, and take a look at what sorts of shops you can expect to find.

Traveller's tip

At some point in your trip to Italy, you're bound to fancy a saunter around the shops to see what's on offer and perhaps pick up a bargain.

The first thing you'll notice in Italian cities is that whilst large chains are of course present, they are less prevalent than would be the case in other European countries. Whereas the UK, for example, is well-known for having branches of the same shops on every high street, Italy's shopping streets offer plenty of traditional, family-run shops and small businesses.

The department stores that no city centre is without are **Standa** and **UPIM**, where you can get pretty much anything. You'll also see foreign stores like Marks & Spencer, C&A and Habitat, but you'll also be reminded that Italy is the home of international success stories such as **Armani**, **Prada**, **Gucci** and **D&G**.

Another typically Italian shopping experience is a local market, which will sell anything from food to fashionable clothes and shoes. In large cities, markets take place every day and there is usually one in

every area of the city. They are known as **mercati rionali**.

In smaller towns, they will happen once a week. This is where really fresh, local food can be found at reasonable prices, and where the real bargains are!

Opening hours are generally quite long, with most staying open until 7.30pm, or later in tourist areas. Be aware that some smaller shops close for lunch, usually between about 1.00pm and 4.00pm, which reflects the relaxed eating experience we saw in Unit 7.

Whether you're a shopaholic or a retail novice, a dip into the sights, noise and smells of Italian shopping is always a colourful experience.

In this unit we'll be revising some of the structures we met in earlier units, and will look carefully at the language you'll need in order to browse and make purchases.

Ha ...?   Have you got ...?
Cerco ...   I'm looking for ...
Preferisco ...   I prefer ...

 ## Listen up 1

Stephanie is looking to buy a blouse for herself. Listen to her conversation with the shop assistant.

⊙ 54

Words and phrases 1

Cerco ...	I'm looking for ... **Cercare**, is 'to look for' – you don't need an extra word for 'for'. You can also use **vorrei** ...
camicetta *f*	blouse
bianco/bianca	white *m/f*
(di) cotone *m*	(made of) cotton
taglia *f*	size (of clothes, etc.)
medio/media	medium *m/f*
Lo/la posso provare?	Can I try it on?
certo	of course
È un po' piccola.	It's a bit small (for me).

La lascio.	I'll leave it.
Quanto costa?	How much does it cost? (An alternative to **Quant'è?** 'How much is it?')
È un po' cara.	It's a bit expensive.
Ce n'è un altro/un'altra?	Is there another one of them? *m/f*
anche	also
carino/carina	pretty *m/f*
Lo/la prendo.	I'll take it.
Paghi pure alla cassa.	Please pay at the till.

 ## Unlocking the language 1

La posso provare?
La prendo.

La is the word for 'it' when 'it' replaces a feminine singular word, in this case **camicetta**. If you were referring to a masculine item, you would use **lo** instead. **Lo posso provare?**

adjectives

In Unit 4 we learned that adjectives often change their ending depending on the word that they are describing. In this dialogue, **bianco/a** and **carino/a** are examples of this. So how would you make **bianco** plural? We know that the masculine plural ending is **-i** but to maintain the *k* sound at the end, we add an *h* – **bianchi** *byan-kee*. For the same reason, the feminine plural is **bianche**.

posso

'I can'. The verb **potere** ('to be able to/ to be allowed to') is irregular so its parts look quite different from one another. Here are the ones you have seen so far:

posso I can
puoi you can (*informal*)
può you (formal)/he/she/it can
One which you haven't seen yet is **possiamo** – 'we can'.

 ## Your turn 1

Find expressions in the dialogue to convey the following. Then check your answers online at www.collinslanguage.com/click. 54

1. I'd like ....

2. There's this one. ....

3. Can I try it on? ....

4. I'll leave it, thanks. ....

5. Is it cotton? ....

6. I'll take it. ....

Pronunciation Tip

questo, quanto, qui

As is the case in standard English, the letter **q** in Italian always comes in the combination **qu**. The pronunciation is the same as in English, but with shorter and sharper vowel sounds: **qua** = *kwah*, **que** = *kweh*, **qui** = *kwee*, **quo** = *kwoh*

preferisco, preferisci, preferisce, scusi

The pronunciation of **sca**, **sco** and **scu** is *skah*, *skoh* and *skoo*.
sci and **sce**, however, are pronounced *shee* and *sheh* respectively.

preferisco = *preh-feh-ree-skoh*
preferisci = *preh-feh-ree-shee*

It's time to revise the numbers so that we can state and understand 🔊 55
prices. How would you say the following prices? Begin each sentence
with costa (it costs) and end it with euro.

1. 19€ ....

2. 24€ ....

3. 35€ ....

4. 47€ ....

5. 58€ ....

••

Listen to the customers and shop assistants on track 56 and then 🔊 56
answer the following questions:

1. What's the problem in the first example? ....

2. Does the second shopper buy the item? ....

3. What does the shop assistant ask the shopper to do in the third example?
....

Match the English expressions on the left with their Italian translations on the right:

1. I'll take it.
2. What size are you looking for?
3. Can I try it on?
4. It's a bit expensive.

Che taglia cerca?

È un po' cara.

La prendo.

La posso provare?

Listen up 2

Moving on to some different shops, there are more decisions to be made. There are two dialogues on this track. In the first dialogue the female shop assistant is using the polite form of address. Then in the second, the shopper and assistant are comfortable using the tu form. Listen out for the different verb endings.

⊙ 57

66 Words and phrases 2

piatto *m*	plate
quale?	which? what?
preferisco/preferisce	I prefer/you prefer (polite 'you' form)
e cinquanta	and 50 cents – in prices, the word **centesimi** (cents) is hardly ever used.
Glielo incarto?	Shall I gift-wrap it for you? You may sometimes be asked **È un regalo?** (Is it a gift?) so that the shop assistant can gift-wrap it beautifully for you at no extra cost.
Molto gentile.	(That's) Very kind (of you).
scarpe (*f pl*)	shoes
Come paghi?	How are you paying? (informal 'you')

in contanti	in cash. Strictly speaking, foreigners in Italy should have their passport ready when using a credit card in a shop, so the assistant asks for **un documento** – 'some ID'.
Inserisci il codice segreto.	Put in your PIN (lit. insert the secret code). The polite variant would be **inserisca** ... It's also common now to hear **inserisci/inserisca il pin**.
Ecco fatto.	That's it – done.
bellissimo/a/i/e	Gorgeous (lit. 'very beautiful')
Vero?	'Right?' (lit. 'true?')

🔓 Unlocking the language 2

preferisco/preferisce	We've got used to seeing pairs of verb forms, where the one ending in **-o** means 'I' do and the other one means 'you' do e.g. **cerco** ('I look for') and **cerca** ('you look for'). Here's another pair, belonging to the verb **preferire** ('to prefer'). Note the difference in meaning between: **vorrei questa camicetta** ('I would like this blouse') and **preferisco questa camicetta** ('I prefer this blouse')
carino, carina, carini, carine	Whereas the **camicetta** in *Listen up 1* was **carina**, the **scarpe** here are **carine**. It all matches up. You will also have noticed the use of **queste scarpe** for 'these shoes'. Just as 'this' becomes 'these' in English, Italian has a means of denoting plurals: **questo** ('this') becomes **questi** ('these') and the feminine **questa** ('this') becomes **queste** ('these').
Vero?	Italians often use **vero?** ('true?') or simply **no?** at the end of statements to turn them into questions, just like we do in English with the tags 'isn't it?', 'can't she?', 'shouldn't I?' etc. The Italian system is much simpler!
Quanto costano?	'How much do they cost?' You saw **Quanto costa?** earlier, but here we are talking about shoes, so we need the 'they' form of **costare**. 'They' forms always end in **-no**.

Think about the use of bianco, bianca, bianchi, bianche to describe various things as being white. Which would be the correct form in each of the cases below?

1. un piatto ....
2. una camicetta ....
3. piatti ....
4. camicette ....

· ·

Can you say the following in Italian? We're using the polite form: ⊙ 58

1. Which do you prefer? ....
2. Shall I gift-wrap it? ....
3. in cash ....

· ·

Make sure you've understood what is being said in these short dialogues. Look in particular for the following information: ⊙ 59

1. How much is the item in the first exchange? ....
2. How will the second shopper be paying? ....

· ·

Each line below has its words in the wrong order. Use the language you've learned in this unit to reconstruct the sentences:

1. il favore codice per segreto inserisci ....
2. dai documento mi un? ....
3. bellissime queste sono scarpe ....

The main points in this unit were:

1. stating what you're looking for in a shop – **cerco una camicetta bianca**

2. wanting and preferring – **vorrei questa camicetta/preferisco questo pullover**

3. this/these – **questo pullover/questa camicetta/questi piatti/queste scarpe**

4. adjective endings – **carino/carina/carini/carine**

• •

Now see how good your memory is. Thinking about a blouse (una camicetta), how would you say the following?

1. I'm looking for a blouse.

2. I'd like a white blouse.

3. I prefer this blouse.

4. It's pretty.

• •

Complete these sentences with the word in brackets using the correct ending:

1. Vorrei queste scarpe (bianco) . . . . , per favore.

2. Questo pullover è un po' (piccolo) . . . .

3. Questi piatti sono (caro) . . . .

4. La camicetta è molto (carino) . . . .

Choose the correct option to complete each sentence:

1. .... camicette sono bellissime.

   a. Questo   **b.** Questa   **c.** Questi   **d.** Queste

2. Preferisco .... piatti.

   a. questo   **b.** questa   **c.** questi   **d.** queste

3. .... pullover è carino.

   a. Questo   **b.** Questa   **c.** Questi   **d.** Queste

4. Vorrei .... camicetta.

   a. questo   **b.** questa   **c.** questi   **d.** queste

Un po' di cultura
A bit of culture

9

We'll take a trip to an Italian museum, looking at what's on offer, what you can expect to pay, and how to say what you need to say there.

In this unit we'll learn two new structures: saying that we're going to do something, and that we would like to do something.

Vado a visitare ...	I'm going to visit ...
Vorrei andare a ...	I'd like to go to ...

We'll also have a closer look at how to say that you like something:

Mi piace ...	I like ...

 Listen up 1

A tourist is at the hotel reception asking advice about a museum. Listen to the conversation and see how much you can understand.

⊙ 60

Words and phrases 1

Vorrei andare/Vuole andare?	I'd like to go/Do you want to go?
museo *m*	museum
arte *f* moderna	modern art
lontano/vicino	far away/nearby (we saw these in Unit 2)
se possibile	if possible. **Se** means 'if'.
Certo che è possibile.	Of course it's possible.
ora, adesso	now
Le scrivo.	I'll write it down for you.
istruzioni *f pl*	instructions, directions
oggi	today
foglio *m* di carta *f*	sheet of paper
Le piace ...?	Do you like ...? (polite 'you' form)

Mi piace (molto).	I like it (a lot).
ingresso *m*	admission; entry
sconto *m*	discount
è aperto	it is open
dalle otto di mattina	from 8am
alle sette di sera	until 7pm
vedere	to see
molte cose	many things
Ci va?	Are you going there? (polite form)
stamattina	this morning (short for **questa mattina**)
oggi pomeriggio	this afternoon (literally 'today afternoon')
fare una passeggiata	to go for a stroll

🔓 Unlocking the language 1

Vorrei andare/ vedere …

'I'd like to go/see …' Up to now, we've seen the form **vorrei** used with an item – **vorrei un gelato** ('I'd like an ice cream'). You can also use it with another verb to state what you'd like to do – **vorrei andare** ('I'd like to go'); **vorrei vedere** ('I'd like to see'); **vorrei sapere** ('I'd like to know'). To make this construction, use the dictionary form of the second verb – it will end in **-re**.

Vado a fare una passeggiata.

'I'm going for a stroll.' You can talk about where you're going by using the structure **vado a** ('I'm going to') + the dictionary form of another verb, e.g. **vado a prendere un caffè** ('I'm going to get a coffee'), **vado a visitare un museo** ('I'm going to visit a museum').

Ora le scrivo.

There is no need to use a future tense in Italian for something which is going to happen immediately. Instead you can just use the present tense. So, **ora le scrivo** (lit. 'now for you I write') really means 'I'll write it down for you now' or 'I'm going to write it down for you'.

Le piace …? Mi piace …

We learned about **piacere** ('to please') in the last unit. Did you notice that you usually have to add 'the' before the thing you're talking about – 'I don't like the art', 'I don't like the coffee'. Note also that when you want to say you would like something (or would like to do something) you should use **vorrei** rather than **mi piace**.

Find expressions in the dialogue (track 60) to convey the following phrases. Remember you can check your answers online at www.collinslanguage.com/click. ◉ 60

1. I'd like to go to the museum. ....

2. I'm going to write down the instructions for you. ....

3. That's very kind of you. ....

4. Do you like modern art? ....

5. Yes, I like it a lot. ....

6. There's a discount with this card. ....

7. Now I'm going for a stroll. ....

Pronunciation Tip

ho, hai, ha

Note that the letter **h** in Italian is used in writing, but is never pronounced. So the words **ho** ('I have') and **ha** ('you have') are in fact pronounced *oh* and *ah* respectively. The same is true for all words beginning with h.

Let's have a look at the new structures we've learned in Unlocking the language 1 above. How would you say the following? There are some hints provided in brackets. ◉ 61

1. I'd like to go to the art gallery. (alla pinacoteca) ....

2. I'm going to have a glass of wine. (prendere un bicchiere di vino) ....

3. I like art. (l'arte) ....

Listen to the voices, and make sure you have understood what the people are saying. Listen in particular for the answers to the following questions: ◉ 62

1. What does the first person like and dislike? ....

2. Which building is the second person going to visit? ....

3. What is the third person going to go and get? ....

'Quando è aperto?' Match the opening times on the left with the corresponding figures on the right:

1. La Pinacoteca di Brera è aperta dalle nove alle tre.   10.00–7.00

2. La Galleria degli Uffizi è aperta dalle dieci alle sette.   4.00–5.00

3. Il Museo Egizio è aperto dalle otto alle tredici.   9.00–3.00

4. La Cappella Sistina è aperta dalle quattro alle cinque.   8.00–13.00

Cappella Sistina, Rome

Listen up 2

During his visit to a museum, Mike buys his entry ticket, gets some assistance from a guide and later strikes up a conversation with another visitor.

⊙ 63

Words and phrases 2

adulto *m*	adult
allora	so/therefore
il venti per cento	20% – notice that you have to include **il** – literally 'the 20%'
fino a	until
contemporaneo/a	contemporary
sezione *f*	section
grande	big

nella sala *f* principale	in the main hall
volantino *m*	leaflet
scultura *f*	sculpture
esperto/a	expert *m/f*
esposizione *f*	exhibition
commento *m*	commentary – it can also mean simply 'comment'
resto *m*	rest (remainder)
poi	then
ci troviamo	'we meet'. Trovarsi here means 'to rendezvous'. So here Carla is saying 'shall we meet at 3pm?'
a dopo	see you later

Unlocking the language 2

andiamo
troviamo

These are verb forms indicating that 'we' are doing the action. **–iamo** is the 'we' ending.

nella sala principale
nell'altra sala

We have already seen that **a** + 'the' (**il, la, lo, l', i, le, gli**) combine to become one word. The same is true of **in** + 'the':

in + il = nel   in + i = nei
in + la = nella   in + le = nelle
in + lo = nello   in + gli = negli
in + l' = nell'

Now that you know these, you will see them everywhere. Whenever you notice one in upcoming dialogues, think about how it is formed.

ci

very often **ci** is used to mean 'there': you have already come across **c'è** ('there is/is there') and **ci sono** ('there are/are there') in previous units, in this unit we have found **ci va?** ('Are you going there?') and **ci vuoi andare?** ('Do you want to go there?'). In some other cases **ci** refers to 'we' and can mean 'us', 'to us', 'each other' or 'ourselves', as in **ci troviamo** , 'we meet each other', 'we'll rendezvous'

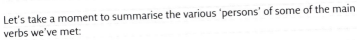

Verbs

Let's take a moment to summarise the various 'persons' of some of the main verbs we've met:

	I	you (**tu**)	you (**Lei**), he, she, it	we	they
essere 'to be'	sono	sei	è	siamo	sono
avere 'to have'	ho	hai	ha	abbiamo	hanno
andare 'to go'	vado	vai	va	andiamo	vanno
volere 'to want'	voglio*	vuoi	vuole	vogliamo	vogliono
preferire 'to prefer'	preferisco	preferisci	preferisce	preferiamo	preferiscono
potere 'to be able to'	posso	puoi	può	possiamo	possono

*You haven't met **voglio** yet because **vorrei** has been used instead. **Vorrei** means 'I would like', so is a little more polite than 'I want'. Look out for **voglio** in the next units – it will crop up from time to time.

 Your turn 2

Use the words to fill the gaps in the passage below. It's an informal dialogue:

è	oggi	c'è	vuoi	troviamo	piace

.... un'esposizione di arte .... al museo. ....
molto interessante. Ti .... l'arte? Se ci .... andare, ci
.... alle undici.

Can you say the following in Italian?    64

1. I prefer sculpture. ....
   ....

2. I'm not an expert. (*it's a man speaking*) ....
   ....

3. Shall we meet here at two o'clock? ....
   ....

Listen to these dialogues. Make sure you've understood what is being said by answering these questions: ⊙ 65

Dialogue a:

1. How much is it to get in? ....

2. What discount is offered with the card? ....

Dialogue b:

3. Until what time is the building open? ....

• •

Each line below has its words in the wrong order. Use the language you've learned in this unit to work out what's wrong:

1. al andare contemporanea vorrei di museo arte ....

2. scultura non un ma sono piace mi la esperto ....

3. un' c'è due alle esposizione ....

◯ Let's recap

In this unit we've looked at what we would like to do, what we are going to do, and what we like. Here are some model sentences to help you remember:

Vorrei andare al museo.

Vado a visitare una galleria.

(Non) Mi piace (molto) l'arte moderna.

• •

How would you say the following, using 'in' + the?

1. in the Museo Egizio ....

2. in the Pinacoteca di Brera ....

3. in the restaurant ....

4. in the main hall ....

5. in the Cappella Sistina ....

Choose the correct option to complete each sentence:

1. C'è il .... per cento di sconto.

   a. grande   **b.** dieci   **c.** questo   **d.** non

2. Mi .... l'arte moderna.

   a. sono   **b.** c'è   **c.** è   **d.** piace

3. .... visitare il museo.

   a. Vado a   **b.** Vado   **c.** Ho   **d.** Andare

4. Vorrei .... molte cose.

   a. essere   **b.** vedere   **c.** museo   **d.** andare

Andiamo alla partita
Off to the football

We'll look at the language you'll need to buy a ticket for an Italian football match, as well as learning something about the country's biggest sporting rivalries!

10

Traveller's tip

Any fixture between AC Milan and Inter Milan is not just a football match – it's a geographical and political battle between two historical rivals. Historically, Milan was supported by the city's working-class and trade unionists, a section of whom were migrants from Southern Italy. On the other hand, crosstown rivals Internazionale were mainly supported by the more prosperous and typically Milanese middle-class.

Equally feisty – and for similar reasons – is any game between Juventus and Turin (both based in Turin) or Rome and Lazio (both in Rome).

You'll struggle to get a ticket for many of the biggest encounters but, on less extreme occasions, it's relatively easy to get a ticket to see a first division match. Many clubs sell advanced bookings on their official websites, but for less prestigious matches you can buy tickets on the day at the stadium or in special kiosks in the city. New anti-violence regulations insist you bring identification that confirms you bought the ticket.

Tickets range from £10-£20 for the **Curva** (the area behind the goals where the hardcore fans tend to set up) up to £80 for **Distinti** and **Tribuna** (the seats along the sides of the field).

The default kick-off time is 3.00 on a Sunday, but TV obligations mean that there are usually a couple of games on a Saturday night (usually starting at around 8.30) and later into Sunday evening. Check in the press or ask at the tourist information office.

Inside the ground, you'll notice that trouble is not that common, and that there is some chanting but far less "singing" than you might be used to. Even for those who would not consider themselves football fans back home, the opportunity to experience a match in Italy is still well worth it. Be prepared to join the rest of the crowd in a cry of **goooool!** when the home team scores!

In this unit we'll be revising some of the structures we've learned in earlier units, including directions, prices and times. We'll also look at a couple of twists on existing verbs, and will be learning some useful exclamations.

Deve ...	You have to ... (polite form)
Per andare allo stadio?	How do I get to the stadium?
Siete inglesi?	Are you English? ('you' plural)

Listen up 1

Tom is a real football fan back home, so he wants to see a match during his holiday in Italy. In these dialogues Tom buys some tickets from a ticket office asks for directions to the stadium and then has a chat with a scarf vendor outside the stadium. See how much you can understand. 66-68

Words and phrases 1

partita *f*	match
biglietto *m*	ticket
in curva	in the area behind the goal
Curva Sud	(behind the) South Goal – geographical points are a common way of denoting an area of the ground
se ce l'ha	if you've got it
in tutto	in total
stadio *m* di calcio *m*	football stadium
deve	you have to
prendere	to take/catch (public transport). Earlier we used **prendere** to order food and drinks – 'I'll have the risotto.'
sciarpa *f*	scarf
Dammi ...	Give me ...

deve prendere

'you have to take' – **dovere** means 'to have to (do something)', or 'must'. Just like in English, it is followed by the infinitive (the dictionary form) of the verb. The forms you'll need are: **devo** ('I must'), **devi/ deve** ('you must'), and **dobbiamo** ('we must'). You met **devo** earlier, in Unit 5.

Per andare allo stadio?

'How do I get to the stadium?' You first met this structure in Unit 3 (**Per andare alla stazione ferroviaria?**). **Per** (lit. 'for') is a very useful word in Italian. Look at all of these other examples of uses of **per**. If you don't remember them, look back at the corresponding unit for a reminder:

Va a Bologna per studiare l'italiano? (Unit 1)

un biglietto per Padova (Unit 2)

la carta per l'assistenza medica (Unit 3)

per dieci notti (Unit 4)

Una birra piccola, per favore. (Unit 5)

Per me, due bruschette al tonno. (Unit 5)

un tavolo per due (Unit 6)

C'è il venti per cento di sconto. (Unit 8)

dammi

'give me'. This is an informal command form of **dare** ('to give'). Don't worry about ordering people to do things in this way – it's completely normal in Italian. You can always add **per favore** if you feel uncomfortable.

Your turn 1

Find expressions in Listen up 1 to convey the following. Afterwards, you can check your answers at www.collinslanguage.com/click.

 66-68

1. To get to the football stadium, please? ....
2. What time is the game? ....
3. I'd like two tickets, please. ....
4. That's 32 euros in total. ....
5. Here on the left, 50 metres away. ....
6. Give me two scarves. ....

Pronunciation Tip

pomeriggio, gentile, gelato, oggi

The letter **g** in Italian acts in a very similar way to **c**, in that it has a variety of pronunciations depending on the letters around it. **Gi** and **ge** are pronounced like the 'ji' and 'je' in the English words 'jinks' and 'jet'. If **gi** is followed by **o** (**gio**) or **a** (**gia**), it sounds like the beginning of 'jot' and 'jacket'. A double **g** means a longer 'j' sound.

singola, guida, paghi, pago, grazie

The **g** in **ga, go, gu, ghi** and **ghe** is pronounced as the '**g**' in the English word 'get'. Any **g** followed by another consonant is pronounced in the same way.

A double **g** means a longer 'g' sound.

Look at the three sentences below, then find their Italian equivalents in the dialogue (track 69). Try to memorise the Italian expressions, then say them out loud: ⊙ 69

1. What time is the match?

2. How do I get to the football stadium?

3. I'd like two tickets, please.

Listen to track 70 and make sure you have understood what the people are saying by answering the following questions: ⊙ 70

1. When is the match in the first example? ....

2. In the second example, how many tickets are bought? ....

3. Which means of public transport is recommended to get to the stadium in the third example? ....

'Dov'è?' Look at the directions and write down the English versions. The map may help you. If you can't remember this vocabulary, go back to Unit 2 to review directions.

a. È in fondo alla strada. ....

b. È a sinistra, a ottanta metri. ....

c. È qui vicino. ....

d. È qui a destra. ....

 ## Listen up 2

Inside the stadium just before the game, Tom and Rachel chat to the man in the next seat. He's a bit older than they are, so they use the polite form.

⊙ 71

Words and phrases 2

Che ne pensa ...?	What do you think ...?
fantastico/a	fantastic *m/f*
siete	you are (plural of **sei** and **è**)
la mia squadra *f*	my team
migliore	better
be'	well
vediamo	let's see
cosa succede	what happens

fuorigioco	offside
Che fai?	What are you doing? (informal 'you')
arbitro *m*	referee
nervoso/a	nervous *m/f*
gol *m*	goal
Non si preoccupi.	Don't worry.
normalmente	normally
segnano	they score
al novantesimo minuto	in the 90th minute
Benone!	Great!
Magari!	If only! Let's hope so!
corner *m*	corner-kick
attaccante *m/f*	striker
pigro/a	lazy *m/f*
in fin dei conti	anyway/at the end of the day
punto *m*	point
ci vediamo ad un'altra partita	see you at another game

Unlocking the language 2

Che ne pensa ...?   'What do you think ...?' A great way of asking someone their opinion on what follows – in this case **dello stadio** (about the stadium)

Che ne pensa dello stadio?   'What do you think of the stadium?' Just as **a** and **in** combine with 'the', so, too, does **di** ('of'):

di + **il** = **del**   **di** + **i** = **dei**

di + **la** = **della**   **di** + **le** = **delle**

di + **lo** = **dello**   **di** + **gli** = **degli**

di + **l'** = **dell'**

Have a look at the CD transcript online at www.collinslanguage.com/click and see how many of these combinations you can spot.

siete	'you are' – the **voi** ('you' plural) form of **essere**. Mario is addressing both Tom and Linda, so rather than **sei** or **è**, he says (**voi**) **siete**. The **voi** ('you' plural) form is not used extensively but you should listen out for it. The usual ending for the **voi** form is **-te**: **volete** ('you want'), **andate** ('you go'), **potete** ('you can').
Magari	A handy little expression, which is flexible enough to mean 'if only', 'let's hope so', 'chance would be a fine thing', etc.

⚓ Your turn 2

Here are some anagrams of Italian words associated with a football match, for you to unravel:

1. tiatrap ....
2. glibteito ....
3. arpcisa ....
4. ratibor ....
5. log ....

....

Can you say the following in Italian? ⊙ 72

1. I want to see a goal. ....
2. offside ....
3. We've got a corner. ....
4. Goal! ....

....

Listen to track 73 in which you will hear four people using expressions you might hear at a football match. Make sure you've understood what is being said by answering these questions: ⊙ 73

1. Which player in the team is mentioned by his number, and what is the speaker's opinion of him? ....
2. Does the speaker like the stadium? ....
3. How many points have we won in the match? ....
4. What is the meaning of the fourth speaker's farewell? ....

The words in each of the statements below are in the wrong order. Use the language you've learned in this unit to work out what's wrong:

1. dello pensa ne stadio che? ....
2. po' un attaccante l' pigro è ....
3. sciarpe favore per due dammi ....

🔄 Let's recap

In this unit we've looked at what we have to do, we have studied the various uses of per and we have also been introduced to plural 'you' endings. Here are some model sentences to help you remember:

Deve prendere la metro.	You should take the underground.
Per andare allo stadio?	How do I get to the stadium?
Siete inglesi?	Are you English?

• •

Now see how good your memory is. Each of the sentences below has one error. Try and spot it, then practise saying the corrected version:

1. Vorrei andare alla stadio. ....
2. La partita c'è alle cinque. ....
3. L'attaccante è bravissima. ....
4. Vorrei due biglietto, per favore. ....
5. Mi piaccio molto la squadra. ....

• •

Add the correct form of 'di' + the:

1. Che ne pensi .... stadio?
2. Che ne pensi .... arbitro?
3. Che ne pensi .... attaccante?
4. Che ne pensi .... museo?
5. Che ne pensi .... mia squadra?

Choose the correct option to complete each sentence:

1. Che ne pensi .... partita?

    a. degli   **b.** dell'   **c.** dello   **d.** della

2. Tom e Linda, ... un po' nervosi oggi, vero?

    a. siete   **b.** avete   **c.** potete   **d.** ci sono

3. Per andare allo stadio, ... prendere la metro.

    a. ha   **b.** deve   **c.** è   **d.** sono

4. Oggi c'è la partita, ... andare allo stadio?

    a. potete   **b.** metro   **c.** essere   **d.** andate

La vita notturna
Nightlife

11

We'll consider some options for extending your days in Italy into the night. Having had an aperitif in Unit 5 and a meal in Unit 6, we'll now be paying a visit to a lounge bar for a nightcap and a bit of live jazz.

Traveller's tip

It is a particularly enjoyable perk of the Italian passion for wining and dining into the wee small hours that restaurants, bars and nightclubs are both plentiful and seemingly always open. In fact, the purpose of Italy's long, sociable evenings is to allow people to unwind gently, unhurriedly, having taken in a good meal beforehand. Eating and drinking generally go hand in hand, and the opportunity to take your time over a drink or two after dinner will undoubtedly make the evening far more enjoyable.

City bars and restaurants will generally start to shut down between 11.00pm and midnight. After this, many Italians will head for **una birreria, un'osteria** or **un pub** – a term borrowed from the English (though pronounced closer to 'poob'). All of these will generally close after 1.00am – sometimes as late as 3.00am or 4.00am – and will allow you to relax with a drink in comfortable surroundings, often listening to live or recorded music.

It's worth noting that in Italy smoking is no longer allowed in public buildings, including restaurants and bars. Some have designated areas for smokers outside.

An evening spent in a friendly Italian bar or club is far more than an opportunity to drink – it is a cultural experience in itself. Watching the local people dance, chat, and unwind in the company of friends will leave you with a lasting impression of the positive effects of a sociable Italian lifestyle – and it will give you the perfect opportunity to practise your Italian!

In this unit we'll be learning the language of making suggestions, and also looking at ways of saying what events are happening.

Possiamo ...	We can/could ...
Perché non beviamo qualcosa?	Why don't we have a drink?
Andiamo a un pub?	Shall we go to a pub?
Ho caldo.	I'm hot.

Katie and Ben are with their new friend Edoardo, and they're wondering what to do after dinner.

A little later on, they're lucky enough to find a bar playing live music.

Remember to go online and check the written transcript if you think it will help with your understanding.

⊙ 74

⊙ 75

Words and phrases 1

Che cosa vuoi fare adesso?	What do you want to do now?
Non so.	I don't know.
Possiamo andare a bere qualcosa.	We could (lit. we can) go and have a drink.
Conosci un locale?	Do you know a place?
Perché non andiamo?	Why don't we go?
d'accordo	OK, agreed
stasera	tonight
musica dal vivo	live music
che tipo di musica	what kind of music
un complesso jazz	a jazz group
comincia	it starts
Entriamo?	Shall we go in?
tavolo *m*	table

banco *m*	bar/counter
gin con acqua tonica/gin-tonic *m*	gin and tonic
con molto ghiaccio *m*	with lots of ice
Gli possiamo ordinare ...	We can order ... for him.
un bicchiere di spumante	a glass of spumante (sparkling wine from Piedmont, in the North West of Italy)
buona idea	good idea

🔓 Unlocking the language 1

Possiamo ...	'We can/could ...' – a standard way of making suggestions: **Possiamo andare a bere qualcosa.** 'We could go for a drink.'
Perché non ...?	'Why don't we ...?' Another way to make a suggestion. Notice that whereas the above option is followed by the dictionary form (**andare**), this phrase uses the 'we' form – **Perché non andiamo?** 'Why don't we go?'
Non so./Conosci un locale?	'I don't know'/'Do you know a place?' In Italian there are two ways to express the word 'know'. **Conoscere** is used when we mean being acquainted with a person or a place. **Sapere** (the dictionary form of **so**) is used when talking about knowledge in general – to be aware of something, or to understand.
Ci sono molti bar e pub	Notice two things here: 1. **molti** changes ending depending on the words that it is with 2. **bar** and **pub** are borrowed from English and thus don't fit into the usual categories for pluralisation – so Italian simply doesn't pluralise them.
Andiamo? Andiamo!	The 'we' ending –**iamo** can also be used to make suggestions. **Andiamo?** 'Shall we go?' **Andiamo!** 'Let's go.' In the dialogue you can also see **entriamo** used in a similar way.

🚀 Your turn 1

Find expressions in the dialogues to convey the following: ⊙ 76

1. What do you want to do now?
2. We could go and have a drink.
3. Do you know a place?
4. There's live music.
5. Shall we go into this pub?
6. We're going to the bar.

Match the names of the drinks with the photos:

1. un bicchiere di spumante
2. un gin-tonic
3. una birra

a.   b.   c.

Pronunciation Tip

birra

The Italian **rr** generally needs a bit of work to be mastered. It's often said that Scots have an advantage here, as their trilled 'rrrr' is what is required. Practise rolling your rr with as many vibrations as you can manage. For extra practice, you could try this tongue-twister: **Arriva correndo il ramarro marrone.** (The brown lizard arrives running.)

How would you say the following? 76

1. What do you want to drink? *(use the informal form)*
2. A glass of sparkling wine.
3. With lots of ice.

Listen to these people talking and answer the questions: 77

1. What does the man want with his gin and tonic? ....
2. What drink does the woman order? ....
3. What is happening tonight, and at what time? ....

Match the suggestions on the left with the activities on the right:

1. Perché non ...?   bere qualcosa, Anna
2. Possiamo ...   entriamo in questo bar
3. Vuoi ...?   a un pub
4. Andiamo ...?   andare al museo se vuoi

Later the same evening, **Katie, Ben and Edoardo are having fun in the jazz bar. Listen to their conversation.**   ⊙ 78

cantante *m/f*	singer *m/f* – **cantante** is both masculine and feminine, but we can see that a female singer is referred to here – **la cantante**
canta	he/she/it/you (polite form) sings – from **cantare**, 'to sing'
carino/a	good-looking *m/f*. We saw this in Unit 8 where it was used to mean 'pretty' when describing a **camicetta** (a blouse).
tesoro	darling (lit. 'treasure').
Perché non ordiniamo ancora da bere?	Why don't we order more drinks? **Ordiniamo** is the 'we' from of **ordinare** ('to order')
O volete qualcos'altro?	Or do you (plural) want something else?
Non voglio niente	I don't want anything
ballare	to dance
Non importa.	It doesn't matter.
Forza!	Come on! (*encouragement*)
bagno *m*	toilet – you may hear various terms for public restrooms: **bagni, gabinetti, servizi, WC, toilette**
ho caldo *m* ho sonno *m*	I'm hot I'm sleepy
sono stanco/a	I'm tired *m/f* – this is used more for bodily weariness; **ho sonno** (see above) refers to feeling sleepy
Chiamiamo un taxi?	Shall we call a taxi?
tornare	to return/go back
a domani	see you tomorrow. **Domani** means tomorrow.

Volete ...?	'Do you want...?' This is the **voi** (plural 'you') form of **volere** ('to want'). Did you spot it?
ragazzo	lit. 'boy'. We already know that this can mean 'boyfriend' but in this case, **ragazzo** is being used to speak directly to someone, in the way that English might use 'mate' or, in the plural, 'guys'. **Forza, ragazzi!** ('Come on, guys'). Crucially, if the recipient is female, the word is **ragazza**!
Ho caldo/sonno.	'I'm hot/sleepy.' A number of expressions that would start with 'I am' in English begin with **ho** ('I have') in Italian. Here we're actually saying 'I have heat' rather than 'I'm hot'. Here's a short list of similar expressions:

Ho caldo – I'm hot   **Ho sete** – I'm thirsty

Ho freddo – I'm cold   **Ho sonno** – I'm sleepy

Ho fame – I'm hungry   **Ho fortuna** – I'm lucky

Chiamiamo un taxi? Ordiniamo una birra?	These are two further examples of the 'shall we' construction we learned earlier in this unit.

✈ Your turn 2

Here are some anagrams of several words and expressions used in the dialogue. Can you solve them?

1. arbella ....
2. neatcant ....
3. bagon ....
4. satcon ....

Can you say the following in Italian?   ⊙ 79

1. I don't dance very well.
2. I'm going to the toilet.
3. I'm sleepy.
4. Shall we call a taxi?

Listen to these people. Make sure you've understood what is being said by answering the following questions: ⊙ 80

1. What is said about the group's singer? ....
2. What solution is suggested to relieve the heat? ....
3. How far away is the hotel? ....
4. When will they next see each other? ....

Look at the questions in the left-hand column, and give the answers on the right. The first row has been completed to start you off. If you need help with the verb forms, use the dialogue or refer back to the table in Unit 9.

1. **Vuoi** una birra?   Sì, ... una birra.
2. **Balli** bene?   Sì, ... voglio .... bene.
3. **Hai** caldo?   Sì, ... caldo.
4. **Sei** stanco?   Sì, ... stanco.
5. **Vai** al banco?   Sì, ... al banco.

 ## Let's recap

In this unit we've looked at various ways of making suggestions. Here are some model sentences to help you remember:

Perché non andiamo a un pub?   **Andiamo a un pub?**

Possiamo andare a un pub.

We also learned some useful expressions to describe your condition using avere.

• •

Now see how good your memory is. Below are some English expressions – say aloud the Italian for each, but in the negative form:

e.g. **I'm sleepy – Non ho sonno**

1. I'm from Rome.   3. I'm thirty years old.
2. I want a glass of sparkling wine.   4. I'm going to the toilet.

• •

Choose the correct option to complete each sentence:

1. .... andare a bere qualcosa.

   a. Andiamo   **b.** Possiamo   **c.** Tu   **d.** Siamo

2. .... non ordiniamo qualcos'altro?

   a. Ho   **b.** Perché   **c.** Per   **d.** Birra

3. Stasera .... musica dal vivo.

   a. jazz   **b.** questa   **c.** complesso   **d.** c'è

4. .... a chiamare un taxi.

   a. Tu   **b.** C'è   **c.** Andiamo   **d.** Hai

Tenersi in contatto
Keeping in touch

12

We'll consolidate what we've learned so far in the course, as well as looking ahead to meeting up with our new Italian friends in the future. To do this, we'll be having a look at the language of modern communication – mobile phones, texting and email.

Traveller's tip

It's great to make friends in Italy during your visit, and to keep in touch once you're back in your own country. It's an ideal way to practise the language, as well as giving you a social foundation for future visits.

These days, your mobile phone – **il telefonino** or **il cellulare** – and email – **la posta elettronica** – are the two most common tools for keeping in touch. In fact, you may already have used email in Italy – in **un punto internet** (internet café – and may be used to phoning or texting home by mobile.

You'll see that Italians are every bit as technologically savvy as foreign visitors are, and that there are a range of telephone companies working in tandem with your mobile service provider back home. Don't be surprised if, when you switch on your mobile on emerging

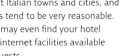

from the airport in Italy, your screen lights up with the name of a local telephone network.

Roaming rates have dropped spectacularly over the last couple of years, but if you want to contact friends and family living in Italy while you're there on holiday, you also have the option of buying an Italian SIM card or even a cheap Italian mobile.

I punti internet can be found in most Italian towns and cities, and rates tend to be very reasonable. You may even find your hotel has internet facilities available to guests.

In this unit we'll be revising questions and answers in the context of making plans for the future, using the language of communication.

Mi mandi un email?	Will you send me an email?
Ti mando un SMS.	I'll send you a text.
Qual è il tuo numero di telefono?	What's your phone number?
Che disastro!	What a disaster!

 ## Listen up 1

Katie and Ben have reached the end of their holiday, and are swapping contact details with their new friend Edoardo before finishing their trip with a farewell drink. Listen to their conversations and see how much you can understand.

⊙ 81-82

 ## Words and phrases 1

Qual è il tuo numero di telefono?	What's your phone number?
Te lo scrivo.	I'll write it down for you.
ci vuole	you need (lit. 'it is necessary')
il prefisso della città	the area code (lit. the prefix of the town)
il mio numero *m* di cellulare *m*	my mobile number
nuovo	new
Non so il numero.	I don't know the number.
Ti do .../Mi dai ...?	I'll give you .../Will you give me ...? (from dare – to give)
il mio indirizzo *m* di posta *f* elettronica	my email address
l'ultimo aperitivo	one last aperitif

qualche	any
delle patatine	some crisps
subito	right away (this was also used by the waiter in Unit 5)
aereo *m*	aeroplane
Vi accompagno all'aeroporto.	I'll come with you (lit. I'll accompany you) to the airport.
Ci andiamo in autobus.	We're going (there) by bus.
è meno caro	it's cheaper (lit. less expensive)
lo stesso	anyway, all the same

🔒 Unlocking the language 1

Qual è il tuo numero di telefono?	'What (lit. which) is your phone number?' Be aware that Italian does not say 'what' but 'which'. Also notice the word order – 'your number of telephone'.
tre, quarantotto, zero sei, novantuno	'3480691'. Digits are stated in pairs – forty-eight, ninety-one, etc. If there's an odd number of digits, the first one is said on its own, then the pairs begin. A pair beginning with zero (e.g. 06) is pronounced **zero sei** (zero six). These conventions take a bit of getting used to, so listen to the dialogue again and focus on how the numbers are given.
il prefisso	'the area code'. To call an Italian landline from abroad you'll need the international code from your own country, then 39 (**trentanove**) for Italy, followed by the town-specific code (**il prefisso**) – for example, this is 06 (**zero sei**) for Rome and 02 (**zero due**) for Milan. Then you continue with the person's number.
la posta elettronica	'email'. Increasingly, Italians are using the English **email** or **una mail** instead.

ben.thompson44@myemail.co.uk	The convention for pronouncing an email address is: ben-**punto**-thompson-quarantaquattro-**chiocciola**-myemail-**punto**-co-**punto**-u-k. The key words here are **punto** for 'dot' and **chiocciola**, meaning 'at'. If you want to say 'all one word', use **tutto attaccato**.
vi accompagno	'I'll accompany you.' **Vi** means 'you' and refers to two or more people (in this case, Ben and Katie). For clarity, compare the following, both spoken by Edoardo: **Ti accompagno, Katie.** **Vi accompagno, Katie e Ben.**
delle patatine	'some crisps' – **di** + 'the' can also mean 'some'.

Your turn 1

Find expressions in the dialogues to convey the following. You can check your answers online at www.collinslanguage.com/click. ⊙ 81-82

1. What's your phone number?
2. I'll write it down for you.
3. Have you got a mobile?
4. I'll give you my email address.
5. I'll come with you to the airport.
6. We can take a taxi.

Pronunciation Tip

città/caffè/perché/è

We've seen several words in this course with a written accent on the last letter. If words are stressed on the last letter, this must be shown by an accent, so the important thing when you're speaking is to emphasise the letter on which the accent is written. Say the words out loud: **cit-tà; caf-fè; per-ché**

How would you say the following? The first two answers are given to get you started:

Il mio numero di telefono è ...

1. 456702 <u>quarantacinque, sessantasette, zero due</u> ....
2. 8456702 <u>otto, quarantacinque, sessantasette, zero due</u> ....
3. 550794 ....
4. 2713601 ....
5. 3162982 ....

Two Italian friends have given you their email addresses, but some of the letters are missing. Try and write down the missing letters as you hear them:

1. pa_l_.ro_ _i@ y_h_ _.i_
2. l_c_a.v_r_ _@con_ _t_ _ _i._ _ _

Questions and suggestions. Match the questions or suggestions on the left with the English translations on the right:

1. Mi dai ...?   Have you got ...?
2. Hai ...?   What's ...?
3. Qual è ...?   We could ...
4. Mi scrivi ...?   Will you give me ...?
5. Possiamo ...   Will you write ... down for me?

Katie and Ben have reached the airport. Now it's time to say goodbye to Edoardo.

 85

Words and phrases 2

dobbiamo	we must, from **dovere**
Mi mandi un SMS/un messaggino?	Will you send me a text? **SMS** and **messaggino** are both common terms. **Mandare** is 'to send'
da Londra	from London
certo	of course
ora ce l'ho	I've got it now
le foto	the photos. Notice that this is plural but there is no s.
Che disastro!	What a disaster!
arrivederci	goodbye
grazie di tutto	thanks for everything
Stammi bene!	Look after yourself/Take care.
Ci vediamo l'anno prossimo.	See you next year. (lit. We see each other next year.)
vi vengo a trovare	I'll come and visit you. (lit. 'I come to find you.') **Vengo** is from **venire**, 'to come'
a presto	see you soon (lit. until soon)
buon viaggio	safe journey

Mi mandi ...? Ti mando ...	Remember that Italian can imply an action in the future just using the simple present tense. What the Italian is literally saying is 'you send me...?' / 'I send you...'. Whereas in English a future tense works best ('will you send me..?' / 'I'll send you...'), Italian keeps it simple by using the present tense.
a ...	In this case **a** literally means 'until'. This is very useful when you want to say 'see you [at some point in the future]': **a domani** ('see you tomorrow'), **a presto** ('see you soon'), **alla prossima** ('see you next time')
Che ...!	This useful construction is a way of saying 'How ...!' or 'What a ...!: **Che bello!** How beautiful! **Che noioso!** How boring! **Che bel vestito!** What a lovely dress! **Che museo interessante!** What an interesting museum!

Your turn 2

Can you remember the expressions needed to construct this short dialogue in Italian? Refer to the dialogue (_Listen up_ 2, track 84) if you need to.

1. Have you got my email address? ....

2. Yes, I've got it. ....

3. I'll send you the photos tomorrow. ....

4. Thanks for everything. ....

5. See you soon. ....

6. Have a good trip. ....

Can you say the following in Italian? They're all fragments of language to do with communication. 86

1. I don't know the number. ....

2. I'll give you my email address ....

3. the area code ....

4. 'dot' (in an email) ....

5. 'at' (in an email) ....

Listen to one person giving an email address, and another giving a phone number. Try and write them both down as you listen: ⊙ 87

1. ....

2. ....

. . . .

Write out these phone numbers in full. We've given you one to get you started:

1. 8231697 otto, ventitré, sedici, novantasette ....

2. 7247642 ....

3. 9183240 ....

4. 5670306 ....

5. 3418299 ....

⟳ Let's recap

In this unit we've looked at various structures to do with exchanging contact information. Here are some model sentences:

Il mio numero di telefono è quattro, ventidue, sessantasette, zero otto (4226708).

Il mio indirizzo di posta elettronica è: anna-punto-terni-chiocciola-italiachat-punto-com (anna.terni@italiachat.com)

We've also learned how to exclaim over something:

Che bello!

. . . .

Now see how good your memory is. Can you remember how to say these phrases?

1. Have you got my address? ....

2. I've got your number ....

3. Two ways of saying 'I'll send you a text' ....

Choose the correct option to complete each sentence:

1. Grazie .... tutto.

    a. di   **b.** per   **c.** con   **d.** in

2. Ci vediamo l'.................... prossimo.

    a. giorno   **b.** anno   **c.** visita   **d.** ora

3. Vi .... a trovare.

    a. voglio   **b.** preferisco   **c.** ho   **d.** vengo

4. .... viaggio.

    a. Buono   **b.** Buona   **c.** Buon   **d.** Buoni

Ripasso 2
Revision 2

Listen up

Remember that in Italian we 'have' an age, rather than 'being' it.
Make sure you can say your age using 'ho ... anni'. Listen to the
voices and write down how old each person is:

⊙ 88

1. Rosa ....

3. Marta ....

2. Paolo ....

4. Federico ....

Tu and Lei

Your use of the informal and polite versions of Italian verbs will depend very much
on what sort of people you're mixing with, and the formality of the situations you
experience. It's a good idea to take some time out and look through all the
dialogues we've covered, practising converting polite verbs to informal, and vice
versa. Remember that in most cases, the informal variant will have an '**-i**' on the
end (e.g. **prendi** – versus the polite **prende**).

For a bit of practice, try changing the following polite forms into informal
versions. The first one is done for you:

Polite	Informal
1. Prende una birra?	Prendi una birra? ....
2. È canadese?	....
3. Va a Milano?	....
4. Ha caldo?	....
5. Parla italiano?	....

Would like to/have to/am going to

Have a look over these structures, and set up a stock of things you can talk about
that you want to do (**vorrei visitare il museo**), have to do (**devo studiare**) and are
going to get (**vado a prendere un caffè**).

Shopping

You've seen that there are a lot of conventions in the language of shopping. Have a look back through the dialogues, and try substituting the items bought for items you'd be likely to buy in Italy. Make a vocabulary list to increase your confidence.

Speak Up

Can you remember how you'd say the following? Try saying the sentences out loud. We are talking about a blouse – una camicetta:

89

1. I'm looking for a white blouse. ....
2. How much is it? ....
3. It's a bit small. ....
4. I'll take it, thanks. ....

Likes and dislikes

Starting with the simple formula of **mi piace…** or **non mi piace…**, you can very easily cover your likes and dislikes. Remember that you don't have to limit this to items or concepts (**mi piace il caffè, mi piace l'arte**); you can talk about activities too (**mi piace studiare**). Asking others about their preferences is easy, too: there's the informal **Ti piace…?** or the polite **Le piace…?**

Communication

Write down all your contact details, then think about pronouncing everything in Italian. It's a good idea to write it all out 'longhand' – e.g. if your phone number begins 348 then write down **'tre, quarantotto'**. This is especially important for your email address: remember the magic words **punto** for 'dot' and **chiocciola** for '@'. Keep practising these until you find you can say them all fluently without referring to your paper, and don't forget the expressions for texting.

In bocca al lupo! (Good luck!)

HAVE YOU SEEN OUR FULL ITALIAN RANGE? PICK A TITLE TO FIT YOUR LEARNING STYLE.

Collins Easy Learning Series

The bestselling language resources, perfect if you're learning Italian for the first time or brushing up on rusty language skills.

Dictionary
£9.99

Grammar
£7.99

Verbs
£7.99

Words
£7.99

Complete 3-in-1 volume
£10.99

Conversation
£7.99

Collins Easy Learning Audio Courses

This exciting course allows learners to absorb the basics at home or on the move, without the need for thick textbooks or complex grammar.

Audio Course stage 1
£9.99

Audio Course stage 2
£12.99

Complete Audio Course (1 and 2) £17.99

Collins products are available from all good bookshops nationwide.
For further information visit: www.collinslanguage.com